YOUR BOOK ON YOUR TERMS

YOUR BOOK ON YOUR TERMS

THE MOST EFFICIENT WAY TO WRITE, PUBLISH, AND PROMOTE YOUR NONFICTION BOOK

JOHN FELDMAN

SPRINGBOARD

PUBLISHING

www.SpringboardBookPublishing.com

Available in hardcover, paperback, and ebook.

For every entrepreneur and thought leader looking to change the world for the better.

CONTENTS

INTRODUCTION

"Lost time is never found again."

— *Benjamin Franklin*

Opening a new book brings so much promise, doesn't it? When you read over the first few lines, you think about what potential it can bring. How it can help you to improve yourself. Your business. Your life.

As a leader and as a creator, you have most likely told yourself a hundred times you need to write a book. *I know it would be helpful*, you've probably said to yourself. With each book you read, you can see yourself on the other end of the deal, penning beneficial words.

But it's the idea of pulling it all together that stops you from moving forward, isn't it? The idea of writing a book strikes often and little bits of information typically trigger that thought, but having enough information for an entire book? You're just not sure. And the time it would take to sit down and figure it out? There's simply not enough room in your busy schedule.

This becomes your roadblock. The overwhelming fear of the unknown turns *I should write a book* into *It would be nice to one day write a book*. Oddly enough, the one thing that separates you from others—being an innovator and a risk-taker—is what's holding you back from accomplishing this task.

So you do what you think is best: *I'll put it on my bucket list*.

Please don't. Don't deprive your potential readers of what you have to offer. Don't allow the lessons you have learned over the years or the techniques you have spent so much time perfecting to go unnoticed due to the (very normal) fear of writing a book.

Think of the people who will continue to struggle to find the information you have. Picture them stumbling through article after article, book after book, taking the time to pick up on little things that they need but always wondering if there is one ultimate source that contains all the information they need.

You can provide them with that resource. And more importantly, *you* can spare them the time they would otherwise spend going down those rabbit holes of information.

What would you have done for a book like this ten, twenty, even thirty years ago?

TIME IS THE ONE COMMODITY WE CAN NEVER GET BACK

The internet is flooded with quotes around this topic. And for good reason—it's true. There is no debating that time will continue to move forward at the same speed, regardless of what we do. We have the ability to dictate how our life will go in nearly every aspect, but time is completely out of our hands.

You understand this already, don't you? As a business owner, regardless of its size, you understand the concept of time. You realize it is the most precious thing we have, and we need to use it as efficiently as possible. That's why you seek out time-saving technology —automation, scheduling, communication. You attempt to find ways to bring more value to the world with what little time you have.

That's why you seek books such as this one, and the many others you have read through and found valuable. You want to learn from others who have been where you aspire to be —let them navigate through the overgrown jungle, carve out a path, and then lead you down that victorious path.

This is exactly what your readers can gain from you.

As the visionary, you are the one who has paved the way. You have filtered out the bad, kept the good, and discovered a path on which one can walk with limited hurdles. You have the information others seek.

By providing your reader a clear path from one point to the next, you save them time they would otherwise spend navigating through the jungle in an attempt to find their own way. Their schedule then opens up and allows them to do more of what they desire to do: create amazing things. Whether it's products, services, events, or any other area of business or expertise, you enable them to move forward unhinged.

THE IMPORTANCE OF BOOKS

By writing a book, you give people the opportunity to change the world. A little dramatic? Maybe. But maybe not. Look at all the innovators in the world and ask yourself how they have been able to accomplish so much.

Elon Musk on how he learned to build rockets: "I read books."

Warren Buffet admits to reading for five to six hours per day, claiming, "That's how knowledge works. It builds up, like compound interest."

Mark Zuckerberg at one point even had his own online book club, where he and the other members read two books per week.

How can busy entrepreneurs like these have so much time for reading? They *make* time, because they understand its importance to their life and to their business.

Think of how books have impacted *your* life. How many have stuck with you over the years? What's the one you're thinking of right now as you read through this paragraph?

That's powerful, isn't it? Think of the fear that must have crept into the mind of the author of that book. Think of the doubt. Think about what your life would be like without that book and how much time you would have spent learning on your own, going through the trial-and-error process.

Your book doesn't have to change the world in an instant. It doesn't have to be read by hundreds of thousands of people to be considered a success. If it helps just one person to become a better leader, creator, provider, supplier, and so forth, then it *can* change the world. It can change *their* world which, in turn, will help to positively change the world of everyone they encounter.

There are roughly 750,000 books published every year. The writing is on the wall, and it's telling us books are not only important, but valued.

THE IMPORTANCE OF THIS BOOK

Similar to your business, ours has a mission, and that's to spread awareness of the ability to write, publish, and promote a book. We want any individual who reads through these pages to know it is possible to write, publish, and promote their book. *The boundaries that once existed have been removed.*

This book is designed to walk an aspiring nonfiction author of any business tier, income level, or societal rank through the steps it takes to write a book. From the initial idea all the way through to publication and promotion, we can help.

At Visionary Literary, we work with clients to write nonfiction books to use as marketing tools. For industry experts and business leaders looking to break into public speaking, coaching, consulting, to boost authority or to create leads, our company helps. But there's a price tag to this. As a marketing tool for your business, that price tag might be well worth it.

After all, you have two payment sources in life: time and money. Your method of payment depends on which you prefer to sacrifice. For most companies, monetary payments to employees and contractors opens time for their senior leadership to work on company growth.

However, some companies might not have a marketing budget large enough at this point to hire a company to take control. This doesn't mean you cannot launch your own book. You have options, and we want to share those with you here. Because, at the end of the day, everyone inside our company is an avid reader, myself included. No, wait. Scratch that. Myself *especially*. I *love* to read. I live for it. My dream is to one day have a library the size of Madison Square Garden and to drive around on a little Segway, grabbing book after book, reading, and retaining as much information as possible.

I'm still far from having enough books to fill a stadium of that size, but I continue to build upon that dream. I read constantly, and I do so because I learn something from every book I read. Each time I open a book and begin to read the Introduction, I can *feel* the author's excitement.

Yet as a ghostwriter for over a decade, I know there were

nerves behind that opening piece. I know imposter syndrome was rearing its ugly head, and the first draft of that Introduction wasn't nearly as prestigious and clean as what was printed on those finished pages.

My goal as a ghostwriter has always been to help the aspiring author: *you.* I want to help you get out of your own head and move swiftly through your writing journey. I have worked with dozens of clients—from former NFL players to leaders of billion-dollar businesses to a World War II veteran (one of the coolest experiences ever)—and I know the struggles. I'm aware of the normal pain points and roadblocks and, more importantly, I know how to help you navigate around those roadblocks.

Yet there is something still more valuable than any of the writing or publishing tips I can offer, and that's the desire to help you save time. You aren't a full-time fiction writer kicking back at your desk and taking the necessary time to structure your book. You're a full-time entrepreneur. A spouse. A parent. A friend. You have obligations.

I founded Visionary Literary after spending over a decade watching authors do things the time-consuming way:

- *Spending up to 40 hours on video calls with your ghostwriter conducting interviews (during business hours).*

- *Having additional calls with your cover designer.*

- *Having additional calls with your typesetter.*

- *Having weekly calls with your project manager.*

- *Having calls to discuss edits and revisions.*

- *Having calls to discuss future calls.*

- *Schedule limitations due to time zone differences.*

- *Working with virtual assistants and executive assistants for scheduling, task completion, and process approval.*

These processes are limiting. They are time-consuming when they don't have to be. Technology in the 21st century is moving so quickly we don't need to use these antiquated models any longer. You have options.

Our goal at Visionary Literary, and through this book, is to help you navigate to the path that's most conscious of your time. We want you to write a professional, earth-moving book, but we don't want you to sacrifice other areas of your life to do so. There's no need for it—not now.

WHY YOU SHOULD WRITE A BOOK

To help.

Because you're not getting any younger.

Because you can.

What's the reason you decided to order this book? The idea had to have done more than just cross your mind, right? Maybe you've been exploring the idea for years, or maybe only a few weeks. Regardless, you probably want to tap into an area that's been restricted but can become available to you once you become a published author:

- **Detailed business card.** Your book can explain, in detail, what you and your business do. Your potential client has choices and by giving them insight into your processes (and your knowledge), you can position yourself as *the* expert.

- **Coaching and consulting.** Want to help people individually? Or in group sessions? The sales pipeline for these services becomes much shorter when you can provide proof of knowledge in a book.

- **Recruit candidates to your company.** What better way to introduce people to your company than to talk about it in a book? Share your core values, what makes you great, why people love working for you, and why your company is in a prime position for continued growth.

- **Raise outside capital.** Doing a funding round? A pitch deck works well but how about giving potential investors a glimpse into what your company does, its history, and its plans for the future inside of an engaging book?

- **Sell a course or mastermind group.** This is one of the most common strategies. Course creators or businesses selling online courses create coinciding books. This helps your business attract potential clients from different sources, and also creates cross-selling opportunities.

- **Speaking engagements.** Want to be a keynote speaker at a conference in your industry or looking to get on a TEDx stage? Proving yourself credible through a book is a near necessity for this.

- **Join advisory boards.** Businesses want true advisors on their board. If you want to gain board seats, prove your knowledge and value through a book. Your authority and credibility elevate the second you hit *publish*.

- **Help others**. You can help yourself and your business, but your book can also change lives. If your book impacts only one person's life and pulls them out of a rough spot, then it can be considered a success.

These are just a few reasons you may want to write a book, but it could be for other reasons as well. You might want to leave a legacy piece for your grandchildren. Or simply document your memoir. Maybe the reason you want to write a book is outside of the norm but fits well into your future plans.

Regardless of the reason, the important thing is you have taken the first step. By opening this book and preparing yourself to learn the tactics necessary to write, publish, and promote your book, you are one step closer to becoming a published author.

Congratulations. You have made it farther than the many others who have talked about writing a book but will unfortunately never do so.

Ready to start hammering away at the keyboard? Anxious to get all your information out into the world? Don't get too anxious. We need to start from the beginning. But I promise, your patience will pay off. As you go through this book and use the resources available through the provided links, I promise you will be in a perfect position to begin.

Let's get started by building the foundation of your book: your *Why*.

PART ONE
PLANNING

CHAPTER 1
KNOW YOUR WHY

"When you know your why, you'll know your way."

— *Michael Hyatt*

THE NEXT FEW months are going to be exhausting. They'll be exciting, for sure, and I'll show you the most efficient ways to complete your tasks, but the process will still take some energy. It will take anywhere from a few weeks to a few months to complete, depending on your schedule and commitment. Writing a book is a project that requires a lot of patience and a lot of resistance to bumps in the road.

But you're used to that, aren't you? You've created something from nothing in the past. If you're reading this book, you have something important to share which means you have already dealt with adversity and come out victorious. My guess is you were able to do this because there was a purpose behind what you were doing. A passion. Your *Why*.

What is the *Why* for your book?

Knowing the reason behind writing this book will help you to face the adversity that is bound to come. It will allow you to overcome obstacles on your path that would normally cause disruption.

If you don't know your *Why* as an author, you will find it far too easy to cave at the first sign of distress. You will close the word processor on your computer or shove your notebook in a drawer and say, "I'll get to it later." Or, worse, you will try to power through the immediate hurdle only to find it leads to a more excruciating editing process down the line. More importantly, an undefined *why* will end up consuming more of your time.

If there's one thing you take from this book—and I know we're early in our journey here—it's that time is precious. Time is our most valuable resource and as a creator and a visionary, you know this. You've put in the long hours to build your brand or your business and you have seen how quickly time can fly by, seemingly wasted, if you let it.

The process I will be walking you through in this book is going to be one that saves time, not wastes it. I know you have businesses to run, families to be around, and a life to manage. Writing a book doesn't have to mean locking yourself in an office for nine months or escaping to some cabin for an entire winter. Those days are gone. We have too many technological features that can help us now. There are too many tools in our toolbox. So many, in fact, that the thing is bursting at its seams.

You can write and publish a book without taking a year off work. You can complete it on your terms and with the professional quality one would expect from a book lining the shelves of any retail store. The only thing you need is the desire to build this puzzle and to be patient when things don't line up right away. Because there will be many times when they won't.

Hence, the reason you must know your *Why*.

WHY WRITE THIS BOOK?

What was the moment that drew you in and made you realize this book needs to be written? Not the moment you decided the book was a good idea, but the one that made you realize it *had* to be written. That it *had* to get out to the world. What caused you to take action and to start looking into ways to write and publish your book?

Remember this reason. Remember where you were, what you were watching, or listening to, or who you were talking to. Think about the emotion you felt in that very moment. Write it down and put it on your vision board. Tape it to your wall. Etch it into your desk. Do whatever you need to do to always have it visible because the going will get tough. There will be points in this process that cause you to hate what you're doing. You will have read over the material so many times and have gone through so many edits that everything will seem utterly boring to you. It will feel as if it's the most jumbled, repetitive piece of jargon you've ever laid your eyes upon, and you'll consider trashing it and scrapping the entire idea of writing a book.

It's true. I have seen it with so many clients. I've had clients with amazing concepts walk away after months of working on something. They needed to be reeled back into their project. They had forgotten about their *why*. Once they remembered their reason for writing their book, they moved on and were able to finish their respective project.

You will struggle at points, but guess what? Even the best writers struggle with this. World-famous fiction writer, Stephen King, once threw his manuscript for *Carrie* in the trash. His wife saw it, took it out, and told him not to give up on it. What happened later? *Carrie* was purchased by a publisher, sold millions of copies, and eventually made into a Hollywood movie.

That book launched Stephen King's career. Imagine where he would be now, had he given up on that manuscript.

Remember your *Why* so you don't end up trashing this project when times get tough. I promise the result will be worth it.

WHY NOW?

Knowing your *Why Now?* will help to support your *Why*.

Timing is important. Are you writing a book on something topical? Did you have the blueprint for a flawless virtual coworking system that kept you afloat during COVID and want to share with others? Are you ahead of the next working trend? Do you have marketing tactics that will help businesses transition into the next five, ten, twenty years?

Why is now the right time to write your book? When you question your *Why* and want to convince yourself to take a break from the book or to cancel its plans completely, you can fall back on the *Why Now*.

WHY YOU?

Why are *you* the right person to write this book? Why are you so passionate about getting this information to the world? Has the information gotten you through tough times you know your reader will go through, or already *has* gone through? What's your unique selling proposition?

This part of the brainstorming process is typically the toughest for aspiring authors. Imposter syndrome kicks in and fear of feeling like you might not have enough impactful information to fill a book makes you reconsider the entire project.

Imposter syndrome affects people in every industry. We all feel as though there are plenty of people smarter than we are, better equipped to relay the message we're working on. It's normal.

Push through it. Remember your *Why*. Know why this book needs to be written.

One way to get over imposter syndrome is to think on a micro level. Don't think about selling millions of copies of your book and hogging the spotlight. Instead, think about the small group of people your book will help. Focus on your niche.

There's a reason you should be the one to share this message. Deep down, you know there is, regardless of any feelings of doubt. You know you have some sort of value to provide to your reader. You know your book can help. Focus on that and don't let it fade.

THESE ARE JUST SAFETY NETS

Alright, let's take a step back here. We have focused on a lot of the potential bumps in the road so far but this is just as a precaution. This is your safety briefing before the roller coaster starts its ascent. It's simply a warning.

Everyone responds differently to fear and anxiety. You may be quick to cut out the difficult processes in your life, or you may choose to take challenges head-on. Both reactions are normal, and you need to be prepared for either.

The idea behind implementing these safety nets early is to ensure you have something to fall back on during difficult times. If you have nothing to fall back on, it will become too simple to move on to the next new, exciting project to tackle and to leave this one behind.

My hope is you see this through to the end. If you do, the reward will be incredible. Think of the day you will hold that book in your hand. Think of your name coming up in search results on Amazon. Think of the feeling you'll have when you schedule your first book signing. Think of the increase in sales and exposure you and your brand will see when you can offer a book as your business card. Think of the first person who will say, "Thank you, this book changed my life."

This process will be a fun one because you have these safety nets in place. Think about it: You're writing a book! This is going to be a great experience. Speaking of which, what are you writing?

CHAPTER 2
WHAT ARE YOU WRITING?

"The first step toward getting somewhere is to decide you're not going to stay where you are."

— J.P. Morgan

IT ALL STARTS WITH AN IDEA. A spark. Your *aha* moment. That's what sent you down the path you chose. While others were taking safer routes, you took a little more risk.

But before you took that risk, you created a plan. Your initial idea might have been first written on a piece of paper or a bar napkin, but it didn't stay there. It grew. That idea expanded into a detailed description, then into a pitch deck, then a business plan, then financial statements, and so forth.

The same steps need to be applied to your book. Some groundwork needs to be laid before your journey begins.

You need to know exactly what it is you want, so you can pursue the correct path.

I want to write a book. To you, that might seem pretty obvious. You want to write something that helps people—something they can order anywhere books are sold online. That's fantastic, but it's still *bar napkin* status. It needs to be clearly defined before any steps toward writing can be completed.

Get up from the bar stool, place the napkin in your pocket, head home, and begin expanding upon the idea.

NONFICTION BOOK CATEGORIES

A book is a book, right? Well, not exactly. It doesn't boil down to just *fiction versus nonfiction.* There are many more components to a book than, simply put, *real or fake.*

When it comes to fiction, there are a seemingly endless number of genres and subgenres. It takes a lot of research to figure out exactly which subgenre your book will fit into, especially if you want it to be successful.

Since this book focuses on nonfiction, that's about as far as I'll go into fiction categories. For nonfiction, however, the level of depth can be just as extensive. Because there are many categories from which to choose. (Fiction has *genres* while nonfiction has *categories.* Same concept, different naming convention.)

- *Religion*
- *History*

- *Philosophy*
- *Children's nonfiction*
- *Education*
- *Travel*
- *How-to guides*
- *Business*
- *Economics*
- *Politics*
- *Memoirs and Biographies*

And the list goes on...

The point is there is a wide range of topics on which one can write. By failing to decipher the type of book you want to write at the beginning, you risk the possibility of working backward in the future—something counterintuitive to opening more of your time.

Which industry are you in? What are you looking to share with your book, and who would be the ideal reader? (*More on Target Audience in Chapter Three.*) These will help you to choose which category is best for you and your project.

Once you determine your category, it's time to think about the voice you want. Don't get too excited, the writing portion won't begin just yet—we're only on the first page of our business plan—but this is an important factor to consider. Your desired voice can help you determine which type of nonfiction book you want to write. And your writing style will help to determine your voice.

NONFICTION WRITING STYLES

Writing is all about painting a picture, right? Maybe. For some types of writing, that's true. For others, not so much.

NARRATIVE NONFICTION

Also called *creative nonfiction* or *literary nonfiction*, this writing style focuses on storytelling aspects. If you want to paint a picture with your words, narrative nonfiction is a writing style to consider.

Shoe Dog by Phil Knight, the founder of Nike, is a memoir written in narrative nonfiction format. It tells a story, painting pictures with its words and driving the reader from one moment to the next with suspense and anticipation, much like a novel would.

This type of writing typically works well with memoirs and autobiographies and is written in first-person format, so the reader is in the shoes of the author.

EXPOSITORY NONFICTION

If you're an expert in your field and you are writing an informative and educational piece, expository nonfiction is the writing style you should use. This lays out the material in a clear, chronological order.

Want an example of a book with expository writing? You're reading it now. This book is designed to walk you through the steps of writing a nonfiction book in a manner that is educational and gives practical advice.

Expository writing works well with business books, educational pieces, how-to guides, and other informative pieces that rely less on painting a picture and more on creating an actionable guide.

PERSUASIVE NONFICTION

Politics, religion, and philosophy tend to be written in this format. Authors writing in this format are looking to persuade others. This writing style provides answers to arguments and is backed up with statistics or other credible findings.

Think of an op-ed piece as an example. The contents of the piece are an opinion, but the reader is trying to make sense of that opinion. There are plenty of political books that can be listed as examples and a simple Amazon search for "political books" can produce a ton of results.

DESCRIPTIVE NONFICTION

Descriptive nonfiction goes further than painting a picture the way narrative nonfiction does. It opens up all five senses. It is narrative nonfiction amplified and is used best in travel guides to portray the surroundings one encounters.

YOUR TARGET READER

More writing options than you thought? Don't be overwhelmed. Most of these you can eliminate right away. And those that seem like a potentially good fit can be analyzed by thinking about the person who will be reading your book: your target audience.

With roughly 750,000 books published each year in the U.S. alone, niching has never been more important. Reaching the masses at the beginning of your book's life isn't possible. The strategy for your book needs to be similar to the strategy for your business: capture the niche market and then expand.

With niching in mind, who is your target reader?

CHAPTER 3

DEFINING YOUR AUDIENCE

"Don't find customers for your product. Find products for your customer."

— Seth Godin

THE NEXT STEP in the planning process is to define your audience. You now know why you're writing your book, but do you know why someone else would read it? More importantly, do you know *who* would read it?

Your writing style will rely heavily on your target audience. Who are you writing this book for? Picture the ideal person who will be flipping through your pages. Is it the same person who would be sitting in the crowd if you were giving a keynote? Is your target audience for the book and for your business the same?

It's important to know who you're speaking to. Great

information written for the wrong crowd will not take your message very far.

The best way to clearly define your target reader is to put together an avatar. Build a character as if you were going to write a fiction novel. Give them a full name, first and last. Choose their birthdate, gender, height, weight, and hair color. Are they married? Do they have children? What is their occupation? Salary? What do they drive? Where do they live? What are their hobbies?

Go deep. Develop this person and then get to know them inside and out. Know what they enjoy and what they don't enjoy. Know what they would want to read, why they would want to read it, and the time of day they enjoy reading the most.

Also, focus on what they *aren't*. What do they *dislike*? What nuances would make them shut the book? These are things you want to ensure you avoid.

DEMOGRAPHICS VERSUS PSYCHOGRAPHICS

Age, gender, where they live, what they do for a living— these are all demographics. The demographics are what sit on the surface. They are easy to spot, which makes it easier to categorize potential readers.

Demographics will be the first you turn to since they are the simplest and quickest to put together. There's nothing wrong with that. Build out the physical description to give yourself a starting point. Then, you can get into psychographics.

It's the psychographics of your target reader that begin to narrow them down and to place them into the niche you're looking to attract.

What interests your target reader? What sort of values do they live by? What defines them and their personality? What sort of information are they looking to consume? These are the psychographics that will help you visualize your target reader.

BUILDING YOUR TARGET AVATAR

When you first started your business and built a business plan, you identified your target market. You placed the demographics—and possibly psychographics—into a person, and you called them your target market.

From there, you built your buyer persona. You created an avatar—a fictional representation of someone who would be a great consumer of your product or partner to your brand. You gave that person a name, a birth date, and a job. Then, you determined whether or not they were in a relationship, had kids, what their salary was, and what their future plans included.

When you created your buyer persona, you created a person you wanted to find in real life, because you knew you had built a product for them.

Think of your *target avatar* as your *reader persona*. They are the fictional person you can create that would greatly benefit from reading your book.

Take a look at the example below, taken from a client whose book is written for retirees looking for investment paths to maintain an income in retirement:

Tom White is an engineer on the brink of retirement. After forty-two long years working in the industry, bouncing from company to company and working his way up the corporate ladder, he has been able to create a nice life for his family. His children are out of the house and as his retirement date approaches, he and his wife prepare for an empty nest.

But they are also preparing for a retirement account that will, for the first time, begin to move backward. For his entire career, Tom has contributed to his retirement funds to set himself up for a joyous retirement but now he's worried. He wants security.

Can you picture Tom White? Does he seem like a real person to you, on the brink of facing real trouble?

This is how you want to build out each of your target avatars—make them real and create a problem that needs to be solved.

PRIMARY, SECONDARY, AND TERTIARY AUDIENCES

Your book can't be targeted toward everybody. Even if it *can* help a general audience, it can't be written with a general population in mind. You need to write it as if you are speaking to your primary audience member.

Is your book about proper nutrition and fitness? That can be for everyone, but you have to choose a primary audience member. *Women between the ages of 21 and 35*, for example. Define your primary audience member, and as you write, envision yourself writing a book for that person specifically.

Your secondary and tertiary audiences are those who would understand the book if they read it, but who the book isn't specifically written for. If you're writing a nutrition and fitness book for a woman between the ages of 21 and 35, your secondary audience member might be her mom. She is closer to the age of 55 or 60, but some of the advice you are sharing can make a positive impact in her life as well.

The idea of selecting your target audience isn't news to you. You have done this with your own product or business, but it must be pointed out here before you begin writing. If you write an entire manuscript, send it to an editor, and they flood your document with red text because they cannot understand who it is you're writing the book for, you're going to start working backward.

And remember, this process is all about being efficient with your time. You have enough to do. Working backward is counterintuitive.

CHAPTER 4
DEFINING YOUR GOAL

"Setting goals is the first step in turning the invisible into the visible."

— *Tony Robbins*

THERE'S one final step to take before starting to put pen to paper. If you're getting antsy, that's okay. But I promise you, all this work up front is going to save you a lot of time and aggravation in the end. You can think of all this preliminary information as your book's business plan. Within that plan lies all this background information pertaining to who you're trying to reach and the message you're looking to get across, but it also lists your goals for the business.

So, what *are* your goals here? What do you wish to see happen with the book? What would make you consider this book to be a successful investment?

Before we move on, let me be as open and honest as possible with you: you shouldn't have the goal to become a New York Times bestseller. This is the go-to response for nearly every prospective author I've spoken with, and it's unfortunate when I have to say it, but the truth is it's nearly impossible to accomplish. And it has nothing to do with the quality of your book. It's much deeper than that.

I'll dive much deeper into the differences between publishing paths in Chapter 14, but to give you some reasoning as to why you shouldn't aim for the New York Times bestseller list, it's because the process is somewhat staged.

To get onto the list, you need to sell about 10,000 copies of your book in the first week of its launch. What most traditional publishing houses do—after they take over all creative control of your book—is they buy 10,000 or 15,000 copies of the book to ensure it hits that bestseller list. Then, they warehouse those books and ship them out as orders are placed.

This will all make a little more sense once we get to Chapter 14 and discuss publishing paths. But for now, as you define your goal, it's important to know there's much more to publishing your nonfiction book than hitting the most notable bestseller list. It would be amazing, sure, and it's definitely something you can strive for, but don't make it your main goal. You'll end up disappointed.

An Amazon bestseller list, however, *is* something achievable. What's better is the Amazon bestselling books are broken up into categories. When your book is number one for a category, it means readers of that category are more likely to see it. Other bestselling lists are extremely generic and throw all nonfiction titles into one basket. Amazon, on the other hand, doesn't. And this can be extremely beneficial when it comes to gaining readership and positive reviews. (More on that in Chapter 20.)

Don't be upset about the reality of the New York Times bestseller list. You don't need book placement in an airport to be successful. You don't need a nationwide media tour for your book to be considered a success. It can still be world-changing for your target reader. It can still positively impact the lives of those who read it.

And if it does? Well, who knows? It could end up spreading like wildfire and maybe you do end up in one of those famous book clubs, on multiple bestseller lists, and on a nationwide media tour. You never know.

THE TRUE SUCCESS OF A NONFICTION BOOK

Book sales aren't going to be your revenue generator. A bit odd to say in a book about writing a book, isn't it? But it's true. It's why most fiction authors struggle to make a living on their craft. They fight and claw their way to capture the attention of readers because that's the only way they can make money. The pool of readers is large, but so is the pool of writers. Remember, there are 750,000 books published each year in the U.S. alone.

Nonfiction is different. We know beforehand that book sales aren't going to generate enough revenue to provide a return on the investment we spent creating it—either time or money. But with nonfiction, you have other options for monetization.

So, how do you see ROI on your book? Whether you pay a full-service company like Visionary Literary, or instead you trade your time and go through the process outlined in this book, there's still a cost to writing a book. You either invest time or you invest money. And you want to see a return on that investment.

This book is a byproduct of your business. It's an extension of you and a marketing tool for your brand. It's okay to desire financial outcomes for your book, but you should have them clearly defined.

What's the overall goal for this book from a return standpoint? If it's exposure for your business, are there certain metrics that need to be hit? For example, if the customer lifetime value in your industry is $20,000, how many customers need to be driven to your business from this book?

Here are some examples of good goals to have for your book:

- *I'd like to have two keynote speaking engagements the year following the book's publication and three to five per year every year thereafter.*

- *I'd like to book one three-day consulting workshop per quarter for each of the next three years.*

- *I'd like to see monthly recurring revenue* (MRR)

increase by one to three percent each month for 12 months following the book's release.

And some not-so-good goals to have:

- *I want to be part of both Reese Witherspoon's and Oprah's book clubs.*

- *I want to be interviewed on The Tonight Show.*

- *Paparazzi should begin to follow me and write up articles about my life.*

The true success of a nonfiction book comes in the form of additional revenue streams. Which one(s) you pursue and the numeric goals for which you strive will determine success levels.

START WITH THE END IN MIND

This is a good rule for writing, but it also applies to goal-setting for your book. Where do you see yourself a year or two after the book has been published? Are you hitting the goals you've listed for your business?

What about the book itself? Will it generate enough buzz? When you attend events and mention the idea of your book, will people generally be interested? Will readers come up to you and tell you it's changed their lives? *I cut out so much of the fat in my business because I read your book!*

Forecasting can help here. Just as you do with your professional life, forecast the future for the book. Think about those moments a year or two from now and come up with the ideal scenarios. Who do you want to impact the most and what do you want the response to be?

How is this book driving your business forward? Plan your goals for the book and start with the end in mind.

CHAPTER 5
CREATING YOUR OUTLINE

"The key to a successful learning environment is structure."

— *Cara Carroll*

HAS your pen been in your hand all this time? A blank legal pad sitting beside you just waiting for ink to start smearing its way across the pages? You've been patient, I know, but the information contained within the first four chapters of this book is the foundation of everything. You need those building blocks to lean on as you begin to structure your book.

With those in place, you can now begin to start formulating your book. Start to gather the ingredients and bring them to the table. In the outline, you will piece all of these ingredients together in a way that gives meaning and purpose to the book you are about to write.

How will your book be structured? Are you telling a story through a character with lessons built in throughout, like Michael Gerber's *The E-Myth*? Are you telling your story through a memoir or autobiography like Phil Knight's *Shoe Dog*? Is your book going to be purely instructional and educational like *Financial Intelligence* by Karen Berman and Joe Knight? Or has your career taught you so many things you'd like to combine your life's lessons through storytelling the way Chris Voss has done in *Never Split the Difference*?

Each of these books is fantastic in its own right. The writing styles vary widely, but they have all been deemed as some of the most influential books to their respective audiences. This is proof there are many successful ways to write a nonfiction book. The important thing is you can connect with your readers and respect their time by providing valuable, actionable advice.

Now is the time to unleash that creativity. Think about how you envision your book. What's the powerful opening hook? How will you structure it from there? What journey will you take your reader on and what will the end result be? What do you want them to do as soon as they read the final page and close the book—what's the call to action?

As you begin to outline, these are questions you should ask yourself.

THE PROCESS IS (SORT OF) OPEN-ENDED

No two writers are the same. Some processes that work well for some authors won't be the best for others. Believe it or not, this is true for a single book project as well. Some processes simply work better for some books while an entirely new process is better for others.

Want an example? My normal process when working with clients is to create a comprehensive outline before I write a single word of the first draft. For me, having every piece of detailed information in the outline allows me to focus solely on capturing the client's voice when I write the first draft. If I know the information is accurate, I don't need to worry about anything else but writing in the client's voice.

I worked with an online course creator on a book recently and went way outside of my normal playbook for the project. Fifteen years of writing one way and I knew it wouldn't be the best case in this scenario. So I ditched my playbook. I didn't even open it. I felt strongly about a new process for this client, and it ended up leading to an amazing result. They were happy, I was happy, and it showed through in the book.

The point is there is no singular method for outlining your book. You need to do what makes you most comfortable. That being said, there are two methods I have found to be the most effective.

OUTLINE METHOD #1: THE COMPREHENSIVE OUTLINE

This is the method we use to work with clients at Visionary Literary. It's the one I have found to be best, and the consensus among clients is that it works. Hashing out all the details before writing a single line of the manuscript makes both parties feel more confident moving forward.

Why does it work? It completely eliminates the roadblocks during the writing process. And with writer's block being such a daunting weight on the shoulders of a writer or ghostwriter, removing its existence leads to higher quality writing, faster results, and happier clients.

The comprehensive outline works in a bulleted method. It's the outline you learned to use in school—the default outline for most word processors and an easy-to-decipher model if using paper.

Here's a brief example of the layout:

1. *Chapter title*
2. *Opening thought (the hook)*
3. *Topic number one*
4. *Details of topic number one*
5. *Further detail—dates, names, information, etc.*
6. *Topic number two*
7. *...*

Is it boring? Absolutely. But is it effective? It sure is.

Let me first tell you why it's been effective for us, as ghostwriters, and then how it can be effective for you.

As a ghostwriter, writing a book for a client who will put their name on the cover, it is a high priority to nail the client's voice. After all, if a friend or family member reads your book, you don't want their first response to be, "This doesn't sound like you." Our job as professional ghostwriters is to take your verbal tone and convert it into written words. The goal is to have the voice in the book so close to your own that you could read the pages aloud flawlessly, without stopping to wonder whether you'd say the words on them.

For us, from this professional standpoint, building a comprehensive outline that contains all the information, in order, with every little detail included does one thing: it allows us to concentrate solely on writing in your voice.

When you write your own book, finding the right tone might not be as important. It will obviously come more naturally to you than it would to a paid writer who has only spoken with you on a number of occasions and listened to just a few short hours of your recorded audio.

Writer's block will still become an issue, though. It's almost a guarantee. When you write at this length, it's inevitable that you will hit rough spots.

Writer's block is one thing, but information gaps are entirely different. They require one of two things. One, you stop, go back and do the necessary research. Or two, you leave a note inside the manuscript to come back to it later. Either way, you're impeding your progress.

Avoid the chaos. Avoid the unnecessary gaps. Work on a detailed outline and have all of that information listed, structured, and clear. It will do wonders for your manuscript when it comes time to write that first draft. It will, hold your breath, be *fun* to write, not a burdening project.

And a quick note here: your outline can, and will, change. Don't get caught up in having the outline written down perfectly. Get something down you are comfortable with, and you can make changes along the way.

Like this outlining style and need a starting point? Pull out your phone, turn on your camera, and scan the QR code below. You will be taken directly to the same template we use for each of our clients. (Alternatively, you can go to www.visionaryliterary.com/diy-resources.) You can use this as your starting point and build on your outline from here.

OUTLINE METHOD #2: THE OVERVIEW PARAGRAPH

Short, choppy outlines aren't for everybody. That's okay. If you prefer long-form explanations to short-form notes, then a paragraph-style outline might be best for you. This format allows you to get everything out in large blocks of text.

The downfall: it isn't as easy to follow along once you begin writing your first draft. Rather than being able to see everything in a clearer fashion—bulleted topics, subtopics, and information—the paragraph can sometimes be stuffed with information in no particular order.

However, this works well for some authors. They prefer to get everything out in paragraph form because the paragraph itself can have some structure, which helps when it comes time to write the first draft of the manuscript. It can also be writing practice for the main event.

Here's how the overview paragraph style of outlining looks, written as if the author of the book is a marketing expert with a company supporting small businesses.

First Chapter:

The reader will be introduced to Angela Adams, the character who is facing struggles in her business similar to the ones the reader is currently facing. Her marketing department is struggling to navigate through the vast sea of advertising opportunities and her business has hit a plateau as a result. She came to our company in dire need of help and she felt like she was alone in her dilemma. Our team let her know that she isn't. In fact, many business owners struggle to get to that next level of marketing. What we have promised Angela is that we can help her to get past those roadblocks by initiating Plan X, Plan Y, and Plan Z, which will be introduced in great detail inside this book. The reader should be prepared to take diligent notes and to put these plans into action.

Second Chapter:

(This chapter will introduce Angela's problems.) Our team sits with Angela at an outside café. The weather is beautiful and it can be said that the energy from the sun and caffeine can't help her. She's disheveled. We listen to her problems and she pours them onto the table. She's shy and doesn't want to be in front of a camera to enhance her social media presence. She also spends thousands of pay-per-click advertising dollars per month but sees little in return. However, she doesn't know if there are any other options. That's when we begin to pull apart her strategy and show her the different paths that she hasn't been able to see. After a long conversation, the exhaustion leaves her face and for the first time since talking to her, there's a glimmer of hope.

Third Chapter:

Angela leaves the meeting with a portfolio...

Notice how the paragraphs are very high level. The detail isn't included because the detail is already highlighted elsewhere. It's in an online course, your business plan, or some other document—maybe it's all stored safely in your head.

For writers who opt into this method of outlining, time seems wasted by writing down all the intricate details because those details can come out in the draft. With the overview paragraph outline structure, you're more focused on how the book will flow—how one thought will move into the next.

You can see why this is something we don't use with clients. Our ghostwriters need more information. We need the granular details and the thorough stories. Without this information, we're at a loss. We don't have your years of expertise and knowledge in our heads. The job of the ghostwriter is to pull all that from you and get it into that first outline example—the comprehensive outline.

THE LENGTH OF YOUR OUTLINE

How long should your outline be? That depends on which outline you choose to use. For the comprehensive outline model we use for clients, a typical outline ranges from seven single-spaced pages all the way to twenty-five pages.

If you're opting into the overview paragraph style, there will be a much wider range for the typical page length. The detail you add and the depth to which you want to explain each chapter's premise will determine the total length of your outline.

There's no right or wrong outline type. Obviously, the longer the outline, the more information you have to work with when writing the first draft of your manuscript. But a short outline doesn't mean you will have a short book, nor does it mean you will have a weak book.

My suggestion? Throw the entire kitchen sink into the outline. It's much easier to cut the fat as you write than to go back into a finished manuscript and add key points. If you find yourself struggling to add content to the book, you can always add case studies, testimonials, visuals, or sidebars to beef up the final page count.

PART TWO
WRITING

THE FIRST DRAFT

"The first draft of anything is shit."

— *Ernest Hemingway*

DID you expect to wait until Chapter 6 to start talking about the first draft? Most people anticipate this as being the starting point of their book. But now you know that isn't true.

All the work we have done to this point was critical. It built the foundation for your book. Now we're ready to properly begin the process you envisioned when you first thought about writing your book: the writing process.

Pull up a chair, get comfy, and block off the next few weeks of your calendar. You're about to get into the zone and have zero distractions while you type away at your keyboard, take breaks to gaze out the window, and create a masterpiece.

Does that sound possible? Of course not. You're busy. You're not a full-time author. You have a business that needs your attention to survive. There's barely enough time in a day for you to stop and eat lunch, so how are you going to block hours upon hours of your schedule to write tens of thousands of words?

This is where the need for ghostwriters has come in—professional writers who will take your outline and turn it into a story for you. A decade or two ago, this process was done by finding a ghostwriter, flying them to your local city or town, putting them up in a hotel, and spending several days with them. The ghostwriter would shadow you as you went about your day, taking notes and when you had a free moment, asking you a question or two to get additional details.

Thankfully, the options since then have become so vast.

It's incredible how much technology has simplified the process, significantly cutting costs while doing so. The cost for a ghostwriter in the way explained above could be mid to high five figures, even as high as $150,000 to $200,000. Yes, you read that correctly. When options were limited and people wanted their books ghostwritten and published, the cost for a top ghostwriter could be that high. And for the few celebrity ghostwriters available today, it still is. For those who are passionate about the traditional publishing route, paying this sort of price could be worth it. (*More on different publishing paths in Chapter 14.*)

Technology and self-publishing options have given way to an entirely new world, opening doors that were typically closed, and dropping costs in the process. For instance, at Visionary Literary, our top-tier package costs $26,000, which is a fraction of the price it would cost to go through the ghostwriting process twenty years ago. While costs in other industries are rising, the writing and publishing industries are getting less expensive. Add to that, the price includes everything: outlining, writing, editing, cover design, typesetting, publishing, and marketing—all of which I'll explain in greater detail as this book progresses.

The point is the options for an aspiring author are far greater than they have ever been. You don't need to be a full-time author, nor do you need to spend six figures hiring one. If you follow the steps outlined in this book, you can be fully committed to your business or work schedule and still write and publish a book.

WHERE TO WRITE

If we're going to talk about how technology has simplified the writing process, we have to start by going through the writing timeline. Historians date the invention of paper all the way back to the year AD 105. Nearly two thousand years ago.

In those two thousand years, nothing seemed to change. Paper quality improved, but there was never any alternative. Manuscripts were written in legal pads, notebooks, binders, and so forth.

A patent for the typewriter was issued in 1868, and it started an entirely new era of writing. Granted, the writing was still done on paper, but the important part is it took 1,750 years of writing on paper, by hand, before something new was invented.

Now, think about the timeline for personal computers. It wasn't until 1974 that this device was invented, and since then, advancements have come much quicker than they had after paper was first invented in AD 105.

The word processor was created by Microsoft in 1983 and now, roughly forty years later, we no longer require keyboards. Dictation services can take care of that for us. Artificial Intelligence can take some key points and write content for us. Technology is truly incredible.

Your options for writing today are vast, but there are a few staples I would recommend using to write your manuscript.

- **Microsoft Word.** This is a staple. It's simple to use, effective, and has dictation tools to allow you to talk into your computer or phone, and the system will write the text for you. You can also download the app onto your phone and work on your project from home or on the go without having to save your file and send it elsewhere.

- **Google Docs.** This has the same features as Word and since it is stored online, you can access it from anywhere. This means you can write from home at night, then head into the office in the morning and work from there without losing your progress.

- **Hemingway App.** This is an online writing tool that allows you to see necessary edits in real-time. If you write a sentence that is difficult to understand, is in passive voice, or contains too many adverbs, the app will notify you right away. Note, however, that this could be a distraction when you are writing your first draft. Instead of using it on your first draft, you may choose to input your content once you've got it all down. Used correctly it's a great writing resource.

GETTING THE WORDS ONTO THE PAGE

Sitting down and getting the words out isn't going to be simple. Your schedule is fluid, changing with the needs of your business and personal life. You know all about sacrificing time to build your business, and if you're writing your book, you will need to tap into this resource again.

But it doesn't have to be daunting. You don't need to spend several hours each night sitting in your office. The writing process can be broken up into short segments, and you can still be making progress.

The way you should monitor your progress is by word count. How many words do you think you can commit to writing every day? (And to avoid becoming disoriented during the drafting process, you should try to write every day.) If roughly 250 words of double-spaced text in a word processor equals one page, how many pages can you commit to writing? How much time do you need to set aside each day to ensure you hit your goal every day?

A good goal to aim for is 500 words. That's two pages of text which, for someone who doesn't write professionally or on a daily basis, might seem like a lot. And it is. But remember, you have laid the foundation for this book already in the form of your outline. The information is there for you. All you need to do is write it in a way that's engaging and understandable.

WRITE FOR YOUR AUDIENCE

Remember who you're speaking to—who you're writing the book for. Empathize with them. Know their current situation. Speak to them in a way that is relatable to *them*, not you. If your book lays out a five-step process for millennials to get their financial wellbeing in order, then don't speak to them as if you're speaking to a lifelong accountant. That's not who they are. It isn't the language they're used to.

As elementary as it may sound, you should try to gear all your writing toward someone in eighth grade. No big, fancy words. You're not looking to impress, you're trying to relay a message. Unless you are world-renowned behavioral economist Daniel Kahneman, you probably won't get away with it. (Kahneman's book, *Thinking Fast and Slow*, is a tough read with lots of large words and complex descriptions, but its contents are incredible and earned him a Nobel Prize.)

Also, remember who the information is coming from—that's you. Keep the tone simple but also make sure it sounds like you. If you're an economist like Daniel Kahneman, a college professor, a medical doctor, or so forth, then my advice to *speak to your audience in a simple tone* might not be appropriate. You might want to aim for a more intellectual piece.

For instance, if you're a medical doctor and your goal through a published book is to gain keynote speaking engagements at seminars and conferences with other M.D.s, you won't want to limit your content. You will need to express your knowledge in a way that is geared toward an audience full of fellow doctors.

DICTATING OVER TYPING

Setting aside time to type 500 words per day might not be doable. To write 500 words, or two full pages, every single day might become too time-consuming. In an era where a 40-hour workweek is a fantasy and work blends into personal life, taking the time to write a total of 40,000 words at a 500 word per day pace might not be possible.

Luckily we live in a time when new technology is created on a daily basis that helps to make our lives easier. One of those technological advances is dictation. Rather than typing out your thoughts, you can now speak them into your phone or computer.

It was only a few years ago that dictating needed to be done through a specific app, or through a dictation microphone. Today, it's available on nearly every writing or texting tool you have at your disposal, including the ones mentioned a few pages back.

More importantly, if time is of the essence, you aren't limited to typing. While the average person's typing speed sits at 40 words per minute, the average number of words spoken per minute is close to 150. If time is a factor and you want to limit how long it takes to pen the first draft of your manuscript, dictating can allow you to finish in less than half the time it would take to type.

An added perk is that many platforms allow you to sync your computer to your phone, so you can switch between dictating while on the road and typing while at home. Without skipping a beat, you can work on your first draft on multiple devices.

While dictating is great, it also needs to be noted that you shouldn't depend on it for editing, or writing a final draft. Spoken writing and typed writing differ. Dictated text can read more like a transcript than a book, so edits will need to be made. But when it comes to that very first draft and getting everything down onto the page and in some sort of cohesive order, dictation can work wonders.

At Visionary Literary, we use dictation software that records audio *and* transcribes it. This way, we can see the transcripts and use them to pull information, but our ghostwriters also have the audio file so they can capture the emotion involved. Doing so saves time for our clients and allows them to record audio at their leisure.

This brings us back to the focus on time and, more importantly, time preservation. It *is* possible to write a book without sacrificing so much time in the process, and it doesn't come at the expense of quality. You have various options available to write your manuscript. And once you have the first draft completed, you're ready to move forward with the editing process.

CHAPTER 7

SUBSEQUENT DRAFTS

"If it sounds like writing, I rewrite it."

— *Elmore Leonard*

THE FIRST DRAFT process allows you to pour your heart and soul into your manuscript. You let everything out, filling page after page until finally, you've come to an end. The sense of pride you will feel at this moment will be incredible.

You will actually be a bit shocked, especially when looking at the word count. *I had tens of thousands of words in me?!* It's a good feeling to have, for sure. And cause for celebration. Once you hit this point in your project, you will have made your way past the crowded *I want to write a book* club and closer to the exclusive *published author* club.

What happens next? What happens after you throw the

entire arsenal out there and everything that was once in your head is now laid out on some word processor? How do you move forward when it seems like you put every bit of information down into this first draft?

First, analyze how the writing process made you feel. Do you feel lighter having gotten it off your chest? Or do you feel vulnerable because all your intellectual property is no longer locked up inside your head?

Both are normal, but also exciting. Having all this information out in a somewhat structured format is the one step most people never complete when they dream of writing a book. However, notice I used the word *somewhat* in there. Because your first draft can be complete, but there's still a lot of work to do when it comes to organization.

Your first attempt is never your final one. Nobody nails it on the first try. You know this from your time building a business. You didn't attain the level of expertise you own today without some pivots in your strategy. You needed to adjust. And like so many successful businesses have done, you may need to pivot your work.

Starbucks launched as a seller of espresso machines and coffee beans. It wasn't until twelve years later that they began to brew and sell coffee.

Instagram started out as an app for people to check in to their location. One of its co-founders called this idea a "false start" before pivoting to an app focused on photo sharing.

"Tune In, Hook Up." Recognize that slogan? That's YouTube's initial slogan, back when they launched in 2005 as, get this, a dating site. Needless to say, they pivoted from that initial idea.

Your book will be the same. It might not need a complete overhaul like Instagram or YouTube. Maybe it just needs to start brewing the coffee it sells like Starbucks. Maybe it just needs a few adjustments here and there—some wording changes, edits to the chapters or subtitles, and some light touching up.

What you need will become clear after you do one thing:

Don't look at the manuscript for an entire week.

It's too fresh. You won't be able to notice any inconsistencies or areas that need editing. You must give it some time. Allow your mind to focus on other things. When that week is over, come back to your manuscript with a fresh set of eyes and get ready to iterate. You will feel refreshed, and the refining process will feel less like a chore and more like an opportunity to improve your creation.

Rarely will you be able to get away with only one subsequent draft to your manuscript. In fact, I recommend doing this week-long pause between each subsequent draft you write. Your final draft will thank you for it.

COMMON CHANGES TO BE MADE IN SUBSEQUENT DRAFTS

If you read through your first draft a week after its completion, you may cringe at some of what has been written. That's okay. Remember, this was your first draft. The goal was to get all the information onto the page in a cohesive manner.

It's inevitable that you will need to make edits to that first draft. While doing so, here are some of the common disconnects that need to be adjusted.

IS EVERYTHING IN PROPER ORDER?

During the first read-through, focus on the high-level context. Are all parts, sections, chapters, and subtitles in the correct order? Are the main concepts of the information you're sharing there?

To make sure you don't get caught up with little edits at this point, you should skim through the entire document looking only at the chapter titles and subsections within each chapter. Think about the order in which they are being told and ask yourself if this is the proper order.

For course creators and educators who have been teaching the process previously, this step may be simple. But for others, this could be a tough task.

If you fall into the latter category, here's a tip: think back to where you were ten or twenty years ago—back before you had familiarity with the topic. Now, if you read through these titles and subtitles in order, with that mindset, is it comprehendible? Does it make sense? Is there a natural flow and fluidity?

This is how your reader will be coming into the book, so it's how you should approach writing it.

THINK OF YOUR READER

Throughout the entire process of writing your book, you must always remember your reader isn't as advanced on the material as you are. They haven't been around it for years and some concepts you have been utilizing for decades could be brand new to them.

Don't assume others know what you're talking about. You see this every day, don't you? Senior leaders inside disorganized companies will reprimand—or even belittle—people in lower roles who misinterpret a task or command. It makes no sense. That person, as the leader and the educator, should be looking in the mirror and asking what it was that *they* missed.

The same goes for your book. This is your strategy—your intellectual property. It's your job to make it clear to others. Make sure the content is written for the person you wish to target. And that person, most likely, does not have your level of knowledge. Quite honestly, if they did, why would they be reading your book?

DO YOU INCLUDE STORIES?

Attention spans are growing shorter. It seems like every new study that comes out tells the story of humans losing the ability to remain focused on one thing.

It's no surprise. There are so many options today that it becomes much easier to abandon what we're doing and move on to something else that seems more intriguing. But you don't want your reader doing this with your book.

Allow them to learn but make it entertaining and engaging; you want to captivate them. Don't allow your book a moment to bore your reader. Keep sentences and paragraphs short and concise. And do what all writers do: use stories or relatable scenarios to allow the reader to have a vision.

Stories can be fictional. For example, you can create a fictional character who is going through the same struggles as your reader. Or you can use real-life case studies to make the learning experience relatable. Facts and guiding points are great to include, but you'll want relatable stories to increase the ability for your reader to retain the information.

The best part? Your reader will retain more information. Storytelling helps people remember things more accurately than learning through simple facts and instructions.

GET IT OUT THE DOOR

At some point, you need to get the manuscript out the door. Otherwise, you will continue to repeat the iteration process forever. When writing long-form content like this, it's impossible to read through and be satisfied with every single sentence. Eventually, you need to admit your book is good enough to get out the door and into the hands of an editor.

How many subsequent drafts should you get through before turning it over to an editor? That depends on how well you build your foundation. Does your outline include everything you need? Did you nail the voice you want for your book by clearly defining your target audience? Did you *remember your why* as you were writing?

The manuscript doesn't have to be perfect at this point. If there are no glaring issues, your editing team should be ready to step in and polish what you have created.

CHAPTER 8

EDITING

"The secret to editing your work is simple: you need to become its reader instead of its writer."

— Zadie Smith

SELF-PUBLISHING GOT its reputation for being amateur because so many writers started to slack off at this point on their journey. They felt as though they had written their book. The hard part was done. *Next up: hit publish.*

But that's not the case.

Look, I get it. Going through the process is a lot of work. Thinking up all the material, organizing it into an outline, writing it down, reading through it, rewriting, re-reading... It's exhausting. Where's the light at the end of the tunnel?

Truth be told, you can't really see it yet. There's a lot more to do. But self-publishing capabilities—while groundbreaking in their own right—don't provide quality analysis. There's no stopping people from taking what they have completed so far, uploading it online, and clicking *publish*.

It will be tempting to do this but please don't. Don't assume your book is *good enough*, especially if you have a business or a brand with its reputation on the line. It's highly advised that anyone wanting to publish a quality book have it professionally edited.

What is editing? It's where you review the book for inaccuracies. This includes more than spelling and grammar. The editing process involves picking out flaws, looking into sentence structure, and finding inconsistencies in descriptions.

As the writer and the owner of this valuable information, you're too close to the project to see these things. You're writing tens of thousands of words and trying to keep everything organized. It's impossible. With long-form content like this, you need the help of others. That help comes in the form of five main types of editing.

THE BASIC TYPES OF EDITING

Yes, there are different types of editing. Five of them, to be exact, although some get combined and used interchangeably. And if I may give you a warning now, you probably aren't going to like the editing process.

Did you enjoy getting highly criticized papers from your high school teacher or college professor? Do you enjoy the thought of seeing red ink smeared across the pages you've written? If so, you're in luck.

But my guess is you're not like that. And that's okay. Neither am I. Still, after fifteen years of writing, I cross my fingers when I send work to an editor and hope it comes back with as little red ink as possible.

Can you guess how often the editorial review comes back with only a single note written on the top saying, "All 200 pages look great!"? The answer: never.

This is why, at the conclusion of the previous chapter, I stressed the importance of eventually *letting your draft go*. Send it to your editor. Get the painful part over with.

Yes, you will feel pain. But your manuscript will thank you for it in the end. As you read and begin to review comments and suggestions from your editor, you will start to realize the work they are doing is beneficial. You will be able to see your writing from a different point of view, and you will be vehemently thanking your editor at the end of the day. (*More on writing Acknowledgements in Chapter 10.*)

Now that you're prepared for what's to come, let's look into the types of edits and how they will be beneficial to your project.

DEVELOPMENTAL EDIT

This is the work you take care of in the beginning. It's the outline you created and the flow of your story. A developmental editor will look at your outline and let you know what they think of its structure. Are there major gaps? Do things not line up?

A developmental editor usually comes in the form of a writing coach or a ghostwriter. At Visionary Literary, this is the first step an author takes when working with their ghostwriter. It starts the process and allows the author to feel confident moving forward.

SUBSTANTIVE EDIT

More can be told about a book once the draft has been written and finalized by an author. If a developmental editor helped you structure an outline, the chances of content topics being out of place are slim.

Having a substantive edit will expose these major inconsistencies with flow and structure before getting too far ahead with other areas of editing. If significant rewrites need to be made, they will be found during this round of editing.

LINE EDIT

A line editor performs—wait for it—a line-by-line edit of your manuscript. Once the structure has been finalized and the macro concept of the book is in good standing, it's time to get micro. It's time to get into the details.

Line edits provide a deeper look into things like sentence structure and word usage. Are you using an active voice? Is your language in line with your target audience? Do you start sentences the same way or are they varied? A line-by-line review will reveal areas that need restructuring.

COPYEDIT

This is the final leg of the editing marathon. It takes place when the manuscript is ready for publication in every other way and needs to be reviewed for correct spelling and grammar.

Also, are you making proper use of sentence structure and your native language? Granted, this isn't your college English essay. It's creative writing. It's engaging. Quick. Punchy. It breaks the rules. The proper way to write is boring and belaboring, and nobody wants to be bored or feel strained when they read. But it may still need some cleaning up.

PROOFREAD

A proofread acts as a backup to the copyedit. If things go unnoticed in the copyediting phase, the proofread should be able to find them.

This is your last leg of defense against the embarrassment of having a typo in your book. As a reader, you've certainly found a typo or two in some books you've read. How did they make you feel? In a book with 100,000 words, a single typo could turn off a reader. Pretty pompous, yes, but it's the truth. You need to acknowledge it and defend accordingly. A final proofread of your manuscript should help.

WHERE TO FIND EDITORS

Luckily, most editors can take care of all five aspects for you —there's no need to find five separate editors. (You should, however, have a different proofreader and editor. A fresh set of eyes is always best when it comes to the proofreading step.)

And, in sticking with the theme of this book, there are plenty of 21st century resources to help you recruit and work with an editor. Here are a few options:

- **Reedsy.** This is a directory of writing and publishing freelancers. It is the go-to site for many writing and editing services. The reason? Each freelancer listed on their site has been vetted, meaning everybody has prior experience and credentials to prove it.

- **ACES.** They are a community of editing professionals who have an Editors for Hire board. Each editor lists their contact information along with relevant experience and the areas of editorial support in which they can assist.

- **Upwork.** It's a little less dependable than the previous two because literally *anybody* can create a profile and list themselves as a professional. But if you take your time and find the right person, it can be great. Also, with Upwork, you create a proposal and editors come to you.

Of course, this isn't the definitive list. There are other ways to find editors: attending conferences, networking with other authors, or joining groups on social media. Twenty-first century tools have made finding a great editor much easier.

HOW NOT TO EDIT

"Mom, can you read this for me?" It's okay to laugh. This is a *terrible* idea. But it's also what many people do when they need someone to read over their work. Heck, this was *my* go-to when I first started writing, back when I was a penniless, aspiring screenwriter. I would hand over my screenplay to anybody willing to give it a read.

What were their responses?

This is amazing!

Wow, you're so talented!

Step aside, Ernest Hemingway!

What ever happened to that screenplay? I buried it. Threw it in the yard and let the wind carry it away, page by page, until the entire thing was separated and spread apart so widely that no human would ever have the chance to lay eyes on the thing in its entirety.

In short, it was awful. But I had no idea. I had asked family and friends to review my work for me, and they did what any family member or friend would do: they lied. They didn't want to hurt my feelings.

Or, worse, they were biased.

Positive reinforcement can do wonders. Having the support of those around you while writing a book is incredibly important, but it can also be bad if those positive responses are the only ones you hear.

Plus, your family and friends can be—and most likely are—your biggest fans. Why show them the early work when you can blow them away with a final book? Hire a professional editor, have your cover design and interior payout completed, and introduce them to the book *when it's actually a book*—not a manuscript in a Word file.

Their level of excitement will be significantly greater, leading to some serious promotional benefits. (*More on this in Chapter* 20.)

THAT BEING SAID... SELF-EDITING OPTIONS

Editors can get costly, and budgets will vary. If you're unable to afford a professional edit, there *are* other ways to ensure your manuscript is in the best possible condition. If you can find and afford an editor, it's highly suggested that you use them. But if you're strapped for cash, don't let that deter you from pursuing your book. Here are some options for you:

LISTEN TO YOUR MANUSCRIPT

Allow your computer, phone, or other software to read your manuscript back to you. You hear errors in this process that you might have missed several times while reading.

- **'Read Aloud' or 'Speak' feature**. Microsoft Word has these options, depending upon your operating system and version you are working within. They are somewhat robotic at the time this book is being written, but they are still valuable.

- **NaturalReader**. This online software has more natural-sounding voices and has different options for reading—mobile or online.

- **Speechify**. It can be used as a Chrome extension, iOS, or Android app and offers various readback features.

USE EDITING SOFTWARE

Technology is great, isn't it? We just discussed software that can read your manuscript back to you and now we're moving into software that can edit it for you. And these options aren't the spelling and grammar edits that we've been accustomed to for over a decade. This isn't spell-checking software. I'm talking about software that can help with word usage, writing style, engagement levels, *and* spelling and grammar.

That being said, there's no replacement for the human eye (and ear). These software options should be reviewed cautiously. Don't "accept all" suggested changes without reading through them.

- **Grammarly.** There's a free and paid option. The free option is great for proofreading but if you want to get the best use out of the writing suggestions, the paid option might be worth it. It's much cheaper than a one-time editor and can provide great feedback.

- **Hemingway Editor.** The idea of writing with your target reader in mind was discussed in Chapter 6. The Hemingway Editor takes your writing and lets you know at which grade level you are writing. Are you on par with your target reader? (Remember that big, fancy words slow down your reader.)

- **AutoCrit.** One of the best features in this is the word repetition finder. When you write thirty, forty, or fifty thousand words, you're bound to use word repetition. This software will find it. It also points out pacing issues, passive voice, and other areas considered to be bad writing. It's software seemingly geared towards fiction but that can be

beneficial if your work is narrative nonfiction,
which includes storytelling components.

There are plenty of options available for editing. Whether you chose a human, software, or both, there should really be no reason not to put some serious thought into your editing process. You may be antsy to get your work out into the world, but your future self—your company and brand included—will thank you for the effort you put into editing.

CHAPTER 9

THE FINAL VERSION

"Where you start is not nearly as important as where you finish."

— Zig Ziglar

YOU HAVE DONE everything you possibly can. By this point, your eyes glaze over any time you try to read over the material on the page. You know the contents of your manuscript by heart and you're starting to find it brutally boring. Quite honestly, you think it's terrible.

You're not alone. Every single author goes through this phase. You're not used to reading the same material over and over. You are so used to reading other books from start to finish, going in with anticipation and coming out with some sort of reaction. Then, it's on to the next one.

It's like walking through a haunted house. You wait in line

and the anticipation builds up. Then, you enter, walk through, hope for the best, and have an opinion about the result as you exit. The same goes for reading a book. You hope it contains that one nugget of information that can completely transform your life or career. Whether or not it does will be determined when you close the book.

Your project, however, feels disorganized. By this point, it seems like everything has been reorganized, reworded, and rephrased to the point that it's confusing. As you read through, you notice topics have been moved around and you wonder if the placement is correct. *Wait, wouldn't that work better (here)? Why did we move (topic x) into (chapter y)?*

It's analysis paralysis. You over-analyze to the point where you prevent yourself from being able to move forward. Again, this is normal, but it's also one of the greatest hurdles to overcome. At this point, it's all too common to lose faith in the project and to feel like it's too far from what you'd envisioned to begin with. You may end up feeling like the hole has been dug too deep. There's no going back. The manuscript is too broken to fix.

This is the point where so many authors call it quits. The manuscript file gets shoved into some folder never to be seen again.

When you hit this point, tell yourself this: *I'm designing the haunted house; I'm not the guest walking through.* There's a difference.

As a guest, you're walking in and admiring everything around you. The artwork, the setup, the costumes, the actors, and their placement. You can admire everything because you're seeing it for the first time.

Being the one designing the house holds a much different mindset. You test different ideas for actor placement. You wonder which props will be placed where, and you have an idea as to why each placement matters: the turns, the hidden crevices where guests will find sudden fear the most.

These are all designed by you and in the weeks or months it takes to construct this house, you question every move you make. *Is this really the best placement for this? Should (prop a) be moved to (placement b)? Is everything in the absolute best order to provide the most optimal outcome?*

Writing a book is the same as designing a haunted house. There's so much that goes into a large project like this. So much moving around, questioning, and reorganizing. It's normal to feel lost, like every guest will hate what you have put together. That's part of being a creator.

What you need are beta testers to come into your house. Allow a select few people to walk through what you have put together and to provide valuable feedback. Do this before opening the doors to the public, and you can eliminate the doubts that would otherwise come with your grand opening.

This is done in the publishing industry also. These testers are called beta readers.

BETA READERS

In Chapter 8, I told you that family and friends would be horrible editors. *And I'll say it here again: family and friends will be horrible beta readers.*

A beta reader is a casual reader who takes your manuscript and reads it in the same way they would approach reading a book. They aren't hyper-focused on critiquing things like sentence structure, voice, and so forth. That's the job of the alpha reader: your editor, who reads your work with a critical eye.

Remember this when selecting your beta readers. You don't want people who are too heavily involved in your book or your industry. Don't hand the manuscript over to your co-founder and ask what they think. Or to your spouse or parent. They're too close to you. And, more importantly, they care about you too much to be honest.

You need to rely on your beta readers to provide honest, open feedback. So choose wisely. Ask business associates. Or someone you know is willing to be brutally honest because they know it's in the best interest of the outcome of the book. Maybe that's a business coach. A member of your board. A fellow entrepreneur. A client. Someone in your networking group. Or, better, a person who falls into your target audience.

One tip: Choose a person who reads widely. By handing over your manuscript to someone who admits that they barely read isn't going to help. You need someone who has walked through many haunted houses, enjoys them, and knows what to expect.

BE SPECIFIC WITH YOUR ASK

"Hey, do you mind reading this for me? Thanks. Let me know what you think!"

No. That's not the right approach. What you're doing by simply handing over your manuscript and asking for open-ended feedback is assuming the beta reader knows what you're looking for. That's like handing someone a shirt and saying, "Let me know what you think."

What do you mean, "What do I think?" Are you asking whether it fits? Whether I like it? If it's comfortable? Whether I like the design? What do you want to know?

Your beta readers need some guidance. Along with your manuscript, send them a questionnaire to answer. Don't overcomplicate it. Just ask a few simple questions followed by one final question that allows them to voice any additional points. More importantly, be specific. Don't ask *yes or no* questions.

Here are some examples:

- **At what point in the manuscript did you first feel lost?** This can tell a lot about the structure of your book. Are several beta readers getting lost at the same point?

- ***Which topic (or topics) seem like they could be moved into a better spot?*** Again, are several readers in agreement? Remember, you did a lot of topic juggling in the weeks or months leading up to this point. Did something get misplaced?

- ***At what point while reading did you take your first break?*** Your goal is to capture the reader's attention throughout the book. Knowing when they found the work boring enough to put down is a big indicator that you may need to go in and try to re-engage at this point.

The list goes on. You can ask any number of questions that will stimulate the mind of your beta reader and provide the feedback you are looking for. If you struggle to find such questions, the link/code at the end of this chapter will take you to our Beta Reader Questionnaire form that you can use or simply pull ideas from.

The important thing, once again, is to make these questions clear and to ask in a way that cannot prompt a *yes or no* response. You want valuable feedback, and you will only get it if you pull the answers from your beta reader.

WHAT TO DO WITH THE FEEDBACK

Your questions should invoke some responses you are looking for. Whether you use our form or generate questions on your own, the goal of this beta reader process is to gain feedback from a reader's perspective, not an editor's.

Ideally, you should have less than a handful of beta readers —between two and four is ideal—and you want to look for trends. If you have too few readers, it will be hard to gauge such trends in responses. Yet if you have too many, you open yourself up to too many opinions.

Take the responses from the two to four beta readers and look into them. If there are common trends, it may be easy to make changes. If not, you may need to do a little further investigating.

But these responses aren't absolute. Changes aren't required. This is entirely up to you (and your editor, if you are still working with one.) Review them. Analyze how they compare to your initial concept. Was the true issue the one they pointed out or was it something in prior pages that led to the reader falling off the path?

The responses these readers will give are subjective. Don't feel like every adjustment must be made based on the feedback. At the same time, don't brush off what your beta readers are telling you.

WHERE TO FIND BETA READERS

I gave some examples in the previous pages of where beta readers might be in your everyday life. A business coach, mentor, associate. But your network might not have that large of an outreach. Maybe you're a solopreneur, or you're just getting started creating online courses.

If you need help finding beta readers, here are a few resources:

- **Goodreads Beta Reader Group.** Goodreads is a website (and an app) geared toward connecting writers and readers, so it's no surprise they would have an active group of beta readers willing to help.

- **Join an online writing group.** Meetup.com is a great resource for finding groups in your local area or online. Business networking groups can also be valuable, given that they can help here, with the beta reading process, but also with your business.

- **Fiverr or Upwork.** You will need to pay for these beta readers, but if you struggle to find readers—or if time doesn't allow you to join the other groups—these are good resources.

If you absolutely must use family and friends, make sure you inform them of the process beforehand. Tell them what you need. Hand them your questionnaire, explain the process, and inform them that constructive criticism will far outweigh kindness in this process.

THE NEXT STEP

Once you have your beta reader feedback and choose which pieces to incorporate, go ahead and make those edits. If you want to give the manuscript one more thorough proofread, do so.

After that, you're done. Your manuscript is complete. The house has been built. All your hard work has produced a manuscript that is ready for the world to see.

Next, you turn this polished manuscript of yours into a real, tangible book.

Need some help with formulating questions for your beta readers? You can find the beta reader questionnaire we use with our clients at www.visionaryliterary.com/diy-resources or by scanning the QR code below. Feel free to use it as is or adjust it to your liking.

PART THREE

TURNING A MANUSCRIPT INTO A BOOK

CHAPTER 10
YES, SWEAT THE SMALL STUFF

"May you find inspiration in the big picture, but may you find love in the details."

— *Adrienne Maloof*

THE CONTENTS of your book are the main event. But there's more that goes into the show than the headliner. Opening acts need to take the stage. The crew behind the scenes needs to receive their credit. The audience needs to get more for their money than a simple one-person show.

Additional components of a book can often go overlooked. Or, worse, they can be glanced over and then thrown together like some superficial elements.

If you have taken the time to pour everything into the manuscript up to this point, don't start to disregard components of the book now. The aspects of your book that will be discussed in this chapter could be just as important to your reader as the main content itself. Sure, some readers' eyes will never see these words, but some will. Keep your professionalism intact by putting care and thought into these items.

FRONT MATTER

How often have you flipped open the cover of a book and examined its first few pages? The title sits alone on the first page, followed by a bunch of small print on the next. Then, comes the Dedication, a Table of Contents, possibly a Foreword, then an Introduction or a Preface.

Long story short, there's a lot to it. And yes, you typically flip right through these pages. But think about what you would do if you opened a book and right there on the first page was *Chapter One*.

Your eyes would shoot open. You might shut the book and open it again, looking for lost pages. Maybe you'd turn it upside down and shake it. *Something's missing*, you would say to yourself. You may even question the legitimacy of the book.

It's the Front Matter that's missing. It's the preliminary information put into books that helps introduce the reader to what they're viewing. It might not seem important to the overall message, but if you want a professionally designed book, these are things you need to include.

Your Front Matter doesn't need to appear in this exact order, but this is how most books will look:

- **Blank page.** After opening the cover, the first page is blank.

- **Half Title Page.** The title of your book sits alone, about one-third of the way down the page. This will only include the title, not the subtitle.

- **Frontispiece** or **Title Page.** A Title Page will list both the title and subtitle in the same font and format printed on the book's cover. If you choose a Frontispiece, the entire cover illustration will be reprinted on this page, title and subtitle included.

- **Colophon.** The book's important information is printed on this page. This is where copyright information, International Standard Book Number (ISBN) listings for each format, publisher information, and legal notices are placed.

- **Dedication.** A short, one- or two-line dedication sits alone on this page, about one-third of the way down. It is usually in italicized text.

A foreword is optional but can be helpful if written by the right person. A foreword is a few-page note to the reader from a person other than the author. It introduces the concept of the book and tells the reader why they should listen to the author—that would be you.

It's a credibility booster. Say, for instance, you're writing a book on how to grow and scale a physical product and Sara Blakely writes a foreword for you. That's huge. Her name holds significant weight in the business world. Her words are trusted. If someone was to pick up your book and sees *Foreword by Sara Blakely*, they might be easily persuaded to buy it. They might have never heard of *you* before, but they *have* heard of Sara Blakely and they will trust her opinion.

If you know someone highly regarded in your industry, reach out to them. Ask them to write a foreword. They can write it themselves, or you can write up something and send it to them for approval—a template for them to then edit. At Visionary, we give authors the option to have their ghostwriter pen a foreword that can be sent for review. Since the ghostwriter will be fully aware of the book's context and message by this point, it ensures the most important, alluring pieces of the book are touched on in the foreword.

Know multiple people who have authority in your industry? That's great. Select one to write the foreword and ask others to write a blurb, which we'll discuss in Chapter 12.

After the Foreword comes your Introduction and then your book's content follows. The reader will be guided through the steps you have laid out for them. They will follow along, intently, taking in every helpful bit of information you provide.

When the Conclusion ends and the reader now has read through your call to action (CTA) and they know what their next steps are, they turn the page to see your Acknowledgements.

In the Acknowledgements section, you flip the switch from *knowledgeable expert* to *humble author*.

Here, you thank everybody who has made your path to this point in your career possible. That isn't limited to the book and its publication. It can date back to your childhood and those who helped you to think outside the box—to think like an entrepreneur. You can thank coaches you have had in your life, parents, teachers, mentors, and those who have helped to mold you into the expert—and soon-to-be published author—you are today.

Be sincere but be short. This section is usually anywhere from one to three pages and briefly acknowledges the people who have made this book possible. Think of the rolling credits at the end of a movie or television show. The people who have made the entire production possible are all listed along with their role in the production. Specifics are left out. It's a high-level *thank you* to everybody who has made an impact on your life.

AUTHOR BIO

Okay, now throw that modesty out the window. Modest is good for the Acknowledgements but not the Author Bio. Here, you list your credentials in paragraph form and in third-person. So you wouldn't say *I have founded three companies with three successful exits*. Instead, you would say (*Your first name*) *is the founder of three companies, all of which have resulted in successful exits.*

Be honest. Boast. Tell everyone why they need to listen to you and why the advice listed within this book wasn't just thrown together. Don't let your reader question their decision to move forward with their CTA. Add confirmation of your authority.

Keep this section short. Write it in a similar fashion to your website or company bio. And don't forget to have a picture that matches the personality you are portraying. You can't write a book called *Burn All the Suits* and then have an author photo of you in a suit and tie. It wouldn't fit the narrative.

And don't forget to smile. Unless, of course, you are writing a book convincing people they shouldn't smile.

CHAPTER 11

YOUR TITLE

"A good title is the title of a successful book."

— *Raymond Chandler*

YOU HAVE ABOUT eight seconds to capture someone's attention.

Think about all the work you've done to this point. All the valuable information you've poured into the pages of your manuscript. All the outlining, planning, writing, editing— all of it could end up being overlooked if you don't have an appealing title.

Imagine yourself browsing Amazon for your next read. Pretend you're in the earliest days of your business and you're looking to scale your company. You type *business growth books* into the search bar and over 100,000 results appear. In a perfect world, you would have time to read hundreds of those books. In reality, your time is limited, and you can only choose one.

You begin to scroll through the results. What are you looking for? What catches your eye immediately? The cover is one component, and we'll spend the next chapter discussing its importance, but when it comes to nonfiction the title tells everything. The title teases the reader by telling them how their world can be transformed—how they can benefit.

Your potential readers are out there, but they are searching for your book in a sea of competing titles. When they search, they're being cautious—even skeptical. When on the hunt for the next book, they want to make sure they make the correct choice. After all, time is of the essence. If someone is going to take the time to read your book, they want to know there's value in it.

TITLE

Let's start with the title—the *main* title. Have you been bouncing ideas around in your head? Wondering what the perfect title would be?

Here's the deal when it comes to the title: *make it short, simple, and easy to remember*. Your goal with the title is to be able to say it to another person without them asking you to repeat it or explain the meaning.

Think back to a podcast you listened to where the guest said the name of their book, website, or business, and you couldn't understand a word of it until they spelled it out or enunciated. Imagine how frustrating it must be for that person to clarify their title every time they speak with someone. Every. Single. Time.

You don't want that, do you? Of course not. You want to be able to quickly and easily announce the title of your book. It needs to be short and sweet.

Zero to One

Shoe Dog

Rich Dad Poor Dad

These are short, sweet, and simple. You could easily tell someone the title of one of these books and no second guessing or confused looks would come in response. If you want your book to spread through word-of-mouth marketing, this is critical.

What these examples lack, however, is context. They don't clearly explain what the book is about. But that's perfectly fine. There's no need to focus on context with the main title. That's what the subtitle is for.

SUBTITLE

Subtitles provide the context that's missing in your title. While your title is attention-grabbing and intriguing to your potential reader, the subtitle tells them exactly what they will learn from reading your book.

Zero to One: Notes on Startups, or How to Build the Future

Shoe Dog: A Memoir by the Creator of Nike

Rich Dad Poor Dad: What the Rich Teach Their Kids That the Poor and Middle Class Do Not

The short, snappy titles are supported by their longer, more detailed subtitles. They provide descriptions. With these subtitles attached, the main titles make more sense.

But the subtitle has further importance. It is where keywords start to become important.

USING KEYWORDS IN YOUR TITLE

Keywords will be discussed in greater detail in Chapter 18 when we review book descriptions and copywriting, but their relevance starts here.

Think of your typical online search. You go to a search engine, type in a few keywords, and within a second or two, millions of results appear. How are they found? How does the search engine know which results to put in front of you? It has everything to do with keywords.

E-commerce is the new way of shopping, and you need to ensure your strategy revolves around this face. Ask yourself questions your target reader is looking to have answered. What are key terms your target reader will search for? Are there typical phrases or acronyms in your industry that stand out?

There are plenty of online resources for finding keywords in your industry. You can use a search engine optimization

(SEO) keyword tool like **SEMrush** or **Google Keyword Planner** to do some research into keywords within your industry.

Tread lightly here, though. Especially when it comes to your book's main title. Don't start keyword stuffing with the hopes it will place your book high on search engine results pages. Websites can determine if you're keyword stuffing—meaning you place a bunch of relevant keywords into a title or description, resulting in a phrase or title that makes no logical sense—and you will be penalized for doing so. Amazon, for instance, penalizes this by dropping you farther down the results pages.

Again, more on keywords in Chapter 18, but it's one thing to note here for your title. If keywords are used effectively, your book can benefit.

USING YOUR BUSINESS NAME

If you have a business, course, mastermind group, or so forth with a trademarked or copyrighted name, consider using it. A great branding strategy involves having uniformity across all offerings.

This can work well for people whose business can be explained through their title, or those who have trademarked their business's name. Having your business title as your book title can help with branding, word-of-mouth marketing, SEO, and many other areas of promotion for both your business and your book.

WHERE TO FIND INSPIRATION

Not sure where to start? Go to where books are sold. Online or in-store, your choice. Search for books in your category. Preferably, look at the best-sellers. Are their titles long or short? One word? Three words? Five? Take out your phone and make a note about trends you see.

Then, start observing subtitles. What are some commonly used words? These will be your keywords. Write those down, too, so that you can go to SEMrush or Google Keyword Planner and do some research.

Throw some of your own opinions into the mix as well. Do you have a piece of unique intellectual property you want to add? Is there a catchy, relevant phrase you use inside your business that can work well as a title, or part of a subtitle?

Take all your research, notes, and thoughts and brainstorm. Compile a list of potential titles and subtitles, then test them.

If you've done A/B testing for your business before, you'll know all about this strategy. You take Option A and Option B, release them both and see which performs better over a period of time. Once you narrow titles down, you can try the same thing with your top two or three titles. Run a Google Ad campaign with each of these titles and see what kind of clicks they render. The one that captures the most attention is your winner.

However, it doesn't have to get so complicated. If you already have a starting point or some ideas narrowed down, you can always ask your followers—not your friends and family, but your clients, community, users, etc. Poll the people who are already interested enough in your product or service that they have paid you money in exchange for it. You already know they are your target audience, so let them tell you what they want.

Once you have a title that works, it's time to design the visual component: the book cover.

CHAPTER 12

COVER DESIGN

"Two things remain irretrievable: time and a first impression."

— *Cynthia Ozick*

DON'T JUDGE *a book by its cover.*

Is that even possible?

It's been nothing but words to this point. Words in your outline, words in your manuscript, words in your title. You have been so focused on touching people with your words. Now, it's time to take a step back and think of your reader from a visual aspect.

Your cover is the first impression of your book. It's what will capture the attention of your potential reader and make them stop scrolling (or *strolling,* if in a brick-and-mortar).

Think of your cover like you think of a first date. Appearance holds a significant impact. At first sight, if your date walks in the door with disheveled hair, wrinkled clothes, and tired eyes, you will immediately want to escape. I hope you have a friend at the helm with a fake emergency call planned. You're going to need it.

When book shopping, you aren't stuck in that predicament. The book doesn't have feelings. You won't feel bad rolling your eyes at the horrific sight and moving onto the next option. It's easier to glance right over it and continue skimming through the options.

The same feeling can be had for your book. A sloppy cover design is easily distinguishable. It shows you're not completely committed to your book. And, more importantly, it shows your date—your potential reader—that you don't care enough about your appearance.

More importantly, if your cover is unappealing, the potential reader will think the contents of the book are the same.

WHERE TO FIND INSPIRATION

Similar to a title brainstorming session, searching for the right cover design should begin with your competitors. What do the top-selling book covers look like? What's the layout? What are the trim sizes?

If you work with a professional designer—which I highly advise—you should send them some samples of what you like. Which books really caught your eye? What do you like about them? Share this information with your designer. But you'll need to do a little bit of research beforehand.

There are some common themes to look for when studying book covers:

- **Color scheme.** Are your book colors going to match your company's? What are those? Do you have hex codes?

- **White space.** Unlike fiction, most nonfiction books contain a lot of white space. You want your potential reader to focus on the message.

- **Typography.** Do you have specific fonts you wish to use? You may wish to use the same font(s) you use for your business, especially if the business and book title are the same.

BLURBS

Blurbs were mentioned in Chapter 10 but become more of a focus here in cover design because of their placement. They will typically be placed on the back cover or the inside flap of a dust jacket. They can also be placed in the Front Pages if you have enough. But for the most part, they're promotional tools placed on the cover.

What are blurbs? They're the one- or two-line reviews of your book by reputable companies or individuals. They help to sell the idea of the book and come from sources like L.A. Times, Washington Post, Huffington Post, and other well-known names.

The best blurbs, however, come directly from individuals. Specifically, those who have a presence in your industry. For example, if you write a book about building rockets and Elon Musk writes a blurb that says something like *It took me twenty years to learn everything [author name] has placed in this book,* there's no way a reader who wants to learn about building rockets is going to pass. You wouldn't have to worry about title, subtitle, and cover design if you had a blurb like that. The blurb could sell itself.

Now, take Elon Musk and have him write a blurb for a book about building fences. It wouldn't make much sense. Elon Musk isn't known for building the world's most durable fences. If he was to write a blurb stating *This is the best guide for building fences,* people would shrug their shoulders.

Marketing tip: Blurbs are all about giving the book credibility, but having blurbs by other credible people on your cover can also assist your marketing agenda. By continuously engaging with those who write blurbs, you can drive excitement for the book. Mention these people in the Acknowledgements. Talk to them about the book. Keep them in the loop and allow momentum for the book to grow before its release. When it comes time to ask for the earliest reviews, you know who to reach out to.

WORKING WITH A PROFESSIONAL DESIGNER

This book is meant to walk you through the steps to write and publish a book on your own. Most of the steps you can do yourself.

But there are some that shouldn't be attempted, and this is one of them. Remember, this is the first impression you will make on a potential reader that has hundreds of thousands of other books to choose from.

The good news is it's easier than ever to find a book cover designer. Whether it's an independent designer or a company that offers the service, several options can be found in very little time. Where you go on your designer search depends on your budget, so the choices can vary widely.

TOP TIER – OVER $1,000

If you want the highest quality, it might cost you a pretty penny. But what you get in return is the peace of mind that you're getting an excellent cover. You don't need to worry about whether your design will come back flawed and cheap. Designers who charge in this price range have the proper software and a wealth of experience.

Where to find designers in this range:

- **Behance.** Adobe Photoshop and InDesign are some of the most popular pieces of design software. So when Adobe starts their own platform for artists to demonstrate their work, it's tough to overlook it. Behance is the platform where artists—book cover designers included—showcase their work.

- **Reedsy.** It's the go-to place to hire professionals for all your book creating needs. Cover design is one of them. And every member of their talent pool is vetted for experience.

MID-GRADE - $300 TO $1,000

Having a modest budget doesn't mean you will end up with a modest book cover. There is an internet—an entire world—full of hungry designers ready to move their way into the Top Tier range. You just need to work a little harder to vet them yourself.

Where to find designers in this range:

- **99Designs.** Want to have a contest where designers create covers and you choose the best? 99Designs does this, allowing you to go through a competition until you find the design (and designer) you like. They also have standard packages that don't require the steps a competition takes.

- **Reedsy.** The same resource that can provide Top

Tier designers will have designers in this price range, too.

UP-AND-COMING TALENT - LESS THAN $300

I use the phrase *up-and-coming talent* and not *bottom of the barrel* because not all work done on the sites I'm about to mention are awful. Most of the professionals on these sites are overseas, which turns off a lot of people who want top quality. But they can still offer some gems.

If you're an industry expert or a business leader, it's rare that you would want to go this low on the quality chart. This is especially true for those who value time over all else. If you want to ensure your time isn't wasted taking risks on unproven talent, use a Top Tier or Mid-Grade designer. You won't need to worry about receiving cheap work and needing to start the process over again.

However, these options are still out there:

- **Upwork.** It's been mentioned as a place to get editors and beta readers; now add cover designers to the mix. They are the most popular site for freelancers to place themselves for work, but unlike sites like Reedsy, the talent isn't vetted. Choose wisely. Look for freelancers who the site lists as *Top Rated* or have a portfolio included in their profile.

- **Fiverr.** It's a cheaper alternative to Upwork, but you pay by the project and not by the hour. The idea for Fiverr started years ago when people would do odd jobs for five dollars or less. Five dollars won't get you much now, but you can still find someone to create a book cover for you for fifty or one hundred dollars.

DO-IT-YOURSELF BOOK COVER

I only recommend doing this if you are publishing an e-book only. Book covers can get incredibly complicated. Things like bleed, color, file type, hex codes, spine width, and many other factors come into play.

If you're publishing an e-book only, or e-book and audiobook, **Canva** has some incredible e-book templates from which to choose. You can have a book cover in a matter of minutes if you use these templates. Or, if you're feeling creative, you can use their blank templates and design your own.

Again, though, I would strongly advise against attempting your own book cover for any physical format. The design you come up with might look great in a digital proof, but when it runs through a printer and ends up on the doorstep of a reader, you might be horrified with the outcome.

THE COVERS YOU WILL NEED

Which formats will you be publishing your book? E-book only? E-book and paperback? Hardcover? Audiobook?

The different formats will be discussed more in Chapter 15 but for now, know that this is something important to discuss with your cover designer. They will need to know the dimensions of your book (5×8 or 6×9, for example).

It's also important to know the spine width for both paperback and hardcover. The spine is the smallest part of the book cover that connects the front and back; it covers the binding of the book's pages.

Your final page count will determine your spine's width. So make sure you know the final page count when you speak with a cover designer. And I'm talking about the page count for the final, edited version of your book—after the Front Matter, Foreword, Acknowledgments, and everything else has been created and the Typesetter and/or Interior Designer have finalized their input.

We'll talk about the Interior Design and Typesetting in the next chapter.

A TEMPLATE QUESTIONNAIRE TO USE WITH YOUR COVER DESIGNER

When you work with a cover designer, a preliminary conversation will typically include a questionnaire sent your way. It will ask you questions about your color scheme, design concepts, vector preference, and images of books you admire (from a cover design perspective).

If you want to get a head start on this process, the QR below is what we send to our clients as they head into the cover design process. It can be a guide for you and your cover designer, or simply an introduction to what you can expect and how to begin brainstorming ideas.

Or you can go directly to www.visionaryliterary.com/diy-resources to find the same document.

CHAPTER 13

LAYOUT AND TYPESETTING

"Good visual layout shows the logical structure of a program."

— Steve McConnell

THERE ARE SO many aspects to the interior formatting of your book that go unnoticed to an untrained eye. Margins, headers, font choice, spacing—these are all thought out and carefully incorporated. Without them, your book has no visual structure.

The guts of your book matter. Everything inside the binding —everything you have worked so hard to put together—can have an emotional effect on your reader simply by the way they look. Fonts, margins, images, and text layout can all matter.

Crazy, isn't it? But it's true that the same words on a page can be interpreted differently based on the layout of the page.

Take the paragraph structure I have used in this book, for example. The paragraphs are short—much shorter than the sentence structure you may be used to in business books of the 2000s and earlier.

Why are they broken up in this format? It's a combination of reasons—two, mainly.

The first is what's called a wall of text. This wall appears when a person attempts to read something on their phone and there is no spacing. No paragraph break whatsoever. Just an entire phone screen filled with a long "wall" of text.

Any written material on a phone needs to be broken up into shorter paragraphs to avoid this wall. Screens are small so that doesn't leave much room for long paragraphs. People are more pressed for time today. They won't take the time to read a paragraph of that length. They'll skim.

The second reason content is broken up is that most of the written content we consume today is web content, and most web content is consumed on our phones. Our news and article consumption are no longer taken in via physical, paper media. Web writers know this, and they try to avoid that wall of text.

The new way to format writing is to match what people are used to now: reading on their phones. This type of content doesn't use indented paragraphs. It doesn't use long paragraphs, long sentences, or a complicated vocabulary. Everything is meant to be fast-paced and easily digestible.

Anyone publishing content now needs to be aware of these subtle changes. That includes you and all the different formats in which you choose to publish.

E-BOOK LAYOUT

Ten years ago, getting your text document to read properly on a Kindle or Nook was a daunting task. I remember one of the first e-books I ever published took two people and three clunky laptops sitting around a kitchen table. It took a long time, staying up until the early hours of the morning. Iteration after iteration and every time we would test the format, it would come back with at least one error.

Today, different pieces of software allow you to upload a single document, make a single click, wait roughly three to five seconds, and then have a prepared file for you. No crazy formatting strategies. No learning by fire. Just the click of a button. This is only one of the many enhancements that have made self-publishing a viable option for a quality, professional book.

You can format your book by uploading your entire interior file (don't forget about the Front Matter, Acknowledgments, and About the Author) into one of the following software systems:

- **Reedsy Book Editor.** Sick of hearing Reedsy's name yet? No, neither I nor Visionary Literary have an affiliation with them. They're just a resource that has expanded its list of tools over time, and their book formatting software is one of them. They truly are a go-to resource for the book creation process.

- **Calibre.** Although this is software you need to download to your computer, it still pushes out exactly what you need in a single click.

Each of these pieces of conversion software—and many others available—allow you to choose your desired book format. For uploading to one of the distributors (*more on this in Chapter 16*) who will place your book into digital bookstores (Amazon, Barnes & Noble, Kobo, etc.) you will need a *.epub* file type. The above resources will provide you with that file type, ready to upload for distribution.

PAPERBACK AND HARDCOVER

The interior files for a physical book will obviously be different than that of an e-book. Here, what you see is what you get. If you use *Tab* to indent your paragraphs, then that space will appear on the page. Same goes with paragraph spacing, margins, etcetera, which is not the case for an e-book file.

There are still some complexities, though. For instance, did you know that margins on a page are adjusted in a specific way to keep the text from getting too close to the binding? Nobody wants to read a book that you need to stretch open with force to see the words at the beginning or end of a paragraph.

Here are some of the important factors to consider when creating your paperback and hardcover files:

- **Trim size.** Will you have a 6×9 hardcover and a 5×8 paperback? Using the standard 8.5×11 page size in Word for both won't work.

- **Font options.** Which fonts are easiest on a reader's eyes? Which go well on white paper, and which go well on cream paper? And which paper type will you choose when you go to publish?

- **Widows and Orphans.** Does the final line of a paragraph get cut off on the bottom of one page and transfer over to another (widow)? Or does the first line of a paragraph appear on the bottom of a page and the rest is sent to the next (orphan)?

- **Page breaks.** Are you hitting the *Enter* button twenty times to get to the next page or are you using page breaks?

You might be an avid reader and had never known about many of these things. But they're important. Our eyes are trained to see books a certain way and if anything is misaligned the slightest, it could jump out at your reader.

Don't allow simple typesetting mistakes to make your book look amateur. Remember, you put a lot of work into this project. Don't let little layout errors take away from its impact.

You can find designers to work on the interior files of your book on any of the sites that have been frequently listed in this book: **Reedsy**, **Upwork**, **Fiverr**, etc. If you want to attempt the process on your own, you're lucky enough to be doing so in a time when software can simplify—and speed up—the process. Here's where you can convert your text file into an interior file for your book:

- **Reedsy Book Editor.** Yes, this works here, too. The same program that can generate your e-book can also generate your paperback, hardcover, and PDF version.

- **Vellum.** The software is free to download, but you need to pay to export your files. It is a reputable piece of software, though, and if you want the assurance of properly formatted files, it might be worth the one-time fee.

Once you have your interior files prepared, finalized, and your cover design(s) complete, it's time to share your book with the world. Literally.

PART FOUR
PRESS 'PUBLISH'

CHAPTER 14

PUBLISHING PATHS

"We make a living by what we get; we make a life by what we give."

— *Winston Churchill*

NOW WHAT? You have the files you need in front of you but what do you do with them? Who do you turn to? What are your next steps?

This book is designed for those who want complete creative control. You have been in control of everything to this point, and you will want to retain that control moving forward.

For you, self-publishing is the desired option. But I want to open your eyes to all the possibilities because maybe there's another one that catches your eye. Or maybe you simply want to know more about the industry so you can feel confident in your decision.

TRADITIONAL PUBLISHING

For so long, this was the only option. If you wanted to write a book, you needed a publisher. They were the ones who worked with the printing press, the media outlets, and the bookstores. There was no other way for an author to find success with a book other than going through a publisher, or spending tens of thousands of their own dollars.

Now, technology has allowed anybody with a voice and a message to have the platform to publish. No longer does one need to hang by the front doors of a New York literary agency, begging for the chance to have their manuscript read by executives.

However, traditional publishing has still been able to survive this mass rush to self-publishing. Mostly, because traditional publishing still holds the keys to the New York Times' bestseller list and bookstores. Authors know if they want to be placed on bookshelves at Barnes and Noble and Books-A-Million, they need a contract with a traditional publisher.

TRADITIONAL PUBLISHING PROS

The main pro: you get to tell people you have been traditionally published. Although the stigma of self-publishing is all but gone, there are still those who feel being traditionally published has an upper hand. They shouldn't, for reasons discussed in the next section, but they do.

Another benefit is the up-front advance on royalties. If you are published by a traditional publishing house, you will more than likely get an advance on your book sales. This means the publisher could send you a check for something like $10,000 up front, before your book is even published. If your book won't be released for another year or two, you can have this money beforehand.

However, this is an *advance on royalties*, not a separate payment. This means the publisher keeps 100 percent of royalties up until they recoup that $10,000. After that, the royalty split then goes into effect—it will be listed in the contract you sign with the publisher.

Finally, the best chance to get into bookstores is through a traditional publisher. For years, publishers have worked with bookstores to have books on their shelves. It's a process that dates back many decades, before the internet and before self-publishing. When publishers and bookstores were the only option, they established fruitful relationships.

Now? Well... how they respond over the next five or ten years will decide their fate.

TRADITIONAL PUBLISHING CONS

Publishing houses rely solely on book sales for revenue. For you, as a business owner and an expert in your industry, your book isn't solely dependent upon book sales. Your book creates additional opportunities for you to showcase your talents—speaking engagements, consulting, investment opportunities. You don't need to worry about selling a specific number of copies to see a return on your investment. For you, the ROI comes with the doors that open *because* you wrote a book and *because* you demonstrated your authority.

Since publishing houses focus heavily on book sales, they become highly selective. This makes it difficult to break into, especially for first-time authors.

The process for being accepted onto an editor's list at a traditional publisher is long, antiquated, and exhausting. Before you even begin the process of writing a book, you need to put together a book proposal, which is essentially a business plan for your book idea. To hire someone to write this for you typically costs between $10,000 and $25,000 or more.

Once you have completed this, you need to "shop" it to literary agents. That includes sending fifty, one hundred, or two hundred query letters to agents to see if they will take the time to review your proposal. If someone likes the proposal, sees its upside (again, they only look at potential book sales), and wants to work with you, further meetings will take place and a contract will be signed.

All done from there, right? Not quite.

From there, the process begins again. Now your literary agent needs to start "shopping" your proposal to publishers. And the waiting game begins again.

Again, it's long, antiquated, and exhausting. The process of landing an agent could take anywhere from one month to two or three years. Then, the agent's process of pitching publishers could take another few months to a year. Then, once you sign with a publisher, the time it takes, on average, is another year or two before your book is completed and released.

Does your business move quickly? Traditional publishing doesn't. If your content isn't evergreen—meaning it won't be relevant for a long time to come—your impactful book may be dated before it even has the chance to hit online stores.

The traditional publishing process also requires that you give away equity in your book. Similar to giving away equity in your company, literary agents, managers, and publishers will all require a percentage of your royalties—not to mention the publisher will demand complete creative control over pricing, title, cover design, and so forth.

Are you willing to give it to them? How will that affect your bottom line?

TRADITIONAL PUBLISHING MYTHS

Most people—aspiring author or not—have this vision that landing a book deal with a traditional publisher is a simple process. You think of this great idea, call an editor at a publishing house, get flown into New York and put up in a suite, have a meeting, sign a contract, have a book written, then go on a national book tour with fans and cameras everywhere and your books sitting front and center on the promotional shelves of every bookstore.

Let that fantasy bubble burst and allow the thoughts to

scatter into thin air because none of that happens. Let me list the reasons why...

One, the process to have an editor even look at your book proposal—what you would write before your manuscript—is brutal. They receive hundreds of these in a given week. What makes yours better than the rest? The chances of receiving a rejection letter—or no response at all—are far greater than receiving an acceptance, or even a positive response.

Two, bookstore placement isn't guaranteed. Of all the books a publisher releases, they pick only a select few to pitch to bookstores. Publishers have their sales representatives take a handful of books to bookstores on a quarterly basis to pitch the idea of ordering copies and placing them on shelves.

Three, marketing and public relations (PR) doesn't work like it used to. That big, national book tour? That isn't going to happen. In fact, when it comes to marketing, most publishers won't even consider reading your pitch unless you have a large following already.

They want you to have already put in some of the marketing effort. Their concern is profit from book sales, so if you don't have any social media following or designated fanbase you likely won't get published. You could have the cure to cancer in written words, but if you have no online presence or following they'll pass and look to someone who they know can help generate sales.

The list of myths could go on. For instance, many publishers also build stipulations into their contracts that say they own any additional rights to the book. Will a documentary or a movie be made regarding your strategy? They own it. And how will that work if you go on a keynote speaking tour or begin consulting on a global level with your intellectual property? If you sign with a traditional publisher, make sure the stipulations of the contract are read thoroughly. Not all publishers are conniving, but some could be.

SELF-PUBLISHING

Self-publishing first began in 1979 when *The Self-Publishing Manual* was released by Dan Poynter. It was a good concept, but there were still many hurdles to get over —mainly, printing costs were still high.

Then, in 2004, Sony released its first e-reader, followed by Amazon's Kindle in 2007. Suddenly, self-publishing became much easier because there were no printers involved. No physical books, covers, or dust jackets needed to be created. Everything was digital. Cheaper. More accessible.

Barnes and Noble released the Nook in 2009 and from there, many followed. Kobo, PocketBook, Boox—there are a bunch. Plus, you can now read e-books directly on your phone through these companies' apps.

Self-publishing has now become a viable option for those who dislike the idea of spending so much time querying, interviewing, and hoping an editor will find their idea promising enough—financially, of course—to take on. There are now options that allow independent authors to publish books of the same quality as their traditional counterparts.

SELF-PUBLISHING PROS

Full creative control is the greatest advantage to publishing on your own. The content that goes in the book, timeline for completion, cover design, title, promotion, pricing, marketing—you control all of it. The only approval you may need to seek is that from your Board of Directors.

Full creative control also means you own the rights to everything. Royalty splits don't exist. Rights to documentaries, movies, or shows made based on your book are yours completely. Future books aren't restricted by any sort of *first rights* agreement. Everything is up to you.

You even have control over which platforms get to sell your book. Do you have some long-standing hatred for Barnes and Noble because you have brand loyalty to Books-A-Million? You can choose not to distribute your book to them.

This is just an example. Don't do this. It would be a horrible decision. The point is to emphasize the fact that you make all the decisions—you have complete autonomy. Just as you did back when your business was in its earliest stages and you were the one wearing all the hats, the publishing choices you make when you go at it on your own are yours to make.

SELF-PUBLISHING CONS

Having control of every step in the process also means you are responsible for getting everything done. Using a team or an assistant is fine, but you need to be the one who implements the team and assigns the tasks.

When you're running a business, this isn't easy. You have a long list of other critical tasks on your desk, and the livelihood of your business depends on those tasks.

Self-publishing, if not done properly, can also lead to a poor, low-quality result. We've all picked up a book or two in our lives and thought *what the hell is this?* You don't want that to be your book. High quality covers, professional formatting, and a well-structured book are all possible, but without the help of a publishing team, they could fall into a category of *what the hell is this?*

On that point, not all self-publishing is a solopreneur adventure. You can hire a team to take care of it for you, or you can outsource. That's what we do at Visionary Literary. We're a hired team of writers, editors, designers, publishing experts, and marketing coordinators that help create a high-quality product and keep the target dates on track.

SELF-PUBLISHING MYTHS

No, publishing your own book does not make you an amateur. Self-publishing won't hold you back from getting traditional publishing deals in the future. It isn't an option for e-books exclusively. As you have read so far in this book, self-publishing is a superior option for industry experts looking to build their brand and enhance authority.

The traditional publishing landscape is too slow for the fast-paced world of business. You need access to publishing options that take months, not years. And you're living in the perfect time to have those options.

CHAPTER 15

BOOK FORMATS

"Having only one option is not an option."

— *Anonymous*

UNBOXING your first batch of books is one of the greatest feelings in the world. Am I biased? Maybe. Writing and publishing books has been something I've enjoyed doing for a decade and a half. But think about the weight my excitement holds. After fifteen years, I still get just as excited when I receive a copy of a client's book.

More importantly, in those fifteen years, there hasn't been a single author who shrugged unenthusiastically when they first held a physical copy of their very own book.

But the publishing landscape has changed dramatically since e-books and audiobooks entered the scene. Readers have more options for absorbing your content, and they want you to match their desires.

That's the most important part. Publishing paperback only and expecting someone who strictly listens to audiobooks to switch up their routine is going to leave you disappointed. One of two things will happen: the person won't read your book or they will do so with displeasure, leading to a worse experience and, subsequently, a worse review.

How will people consume the contents of your book? Will they flip through the pages? Remove the dust jacket and keep it as a collector's item? Download the e-book and read while on the go? Different book formats appeal to different readers. The target audience member defined in Chapter 3 will tell you who those readers are, which will determine the best book formats to choose.

Does the content of your book cater to professional rideshare drivers, offering them a formula to increase potential earnings? They'll be on the road all the time, so an audiobook option is a must.

Does your book offer business advice to outside sales representatives always on the move, in and out of airports? A paperback version of your book could be small, lightweight, and easy to transport inside of a travel bag or briefcase.

Empathize with your target audience member. Think about what works best for them. If you need to, run some tests. Ask your following which book format they prefer. Take those results and strategize accordingly.

E-BOOK

I bought my first e-reader ten years ago and I remember thinking to myself, "Wow, this is going to be the end of physical books." I imagined a world where libraries no longer had bookshelves. Instead, they would have a large selection of e-readers at the front door. As a person would enter, they would grab an e-reader that had the entire library's selection downloaded inside.

Futuristic, but also sad to see so many physical books being recycled.

Fast-forward ten years from the time I bought that first e-reader and physical books are selling better now than ever before. However, e-book sales are still a viable, popular reading option for many, especially since e-reading capability is now available on any smartphone.

When you publish a book, choosing to have an e-book option is a no-brainer. The up-front cost is minimal. When e-books first came to the market, the process took hours—even days—to complete. A *trial-and-error* process would be on repeat and, often, e-books that were self-published would be riddled with formatting mistakes.

Software options mentioned in Chapter 13 have changed that. This has allowed professionally designed books to be simple to create and publish, not to mention the time-saving component.

Revenues are also higher for an e-book. For instance, an e-book priced at $4.99 could earn you a higher royalty payment than a hardcover for $26.99. How is it possible? There are no overhead costs associated. No print costs, shipping costs, nothing.

Having an e-book option is a must, but it cannot be the *only* option. I've been continually hammering home the point that self-publishing is no longer seen as amateur, however, publishing e-book only *is* very amateur. It is known both inside the publishing world and out that it's simple to publish e-book only. Anybody—and I mean *anybody*—can write some words on a word processor, design an e-book cover on Canva, and have a self-published e-book.

These are the people who drag the term *self-publishing* through the mud. I understand their desire to publish and to hope that *if you publish, they will come* works for them, but it doesn't. Hitting publish on an e-book and crossing your fingers leads to a listing with no reviews, falling farther and farther down the rankings list as it sits and collects digital dust. (Thinking the *if you build it, they will come* method of publishing will work with *any* format is a bad idea. More on that in Part 5.)

PAPERBACK

In the order of recommended publishing options, the paperback format is next in line. Having this format in addition to the e-book format really brings your book to life. It's tangible. You can hold it, flip through the pages and breathe in that new book smell—things that aren't possible with an e-book.

I mentioned unboxing your books in the opening of this chapter because it's what anyone thinks of when they think of publishing a book: peeling open that cardboard box and seeing a stack of your covers looking up at you.

Believe me, that feeling never gets old. But there's more to it than the excitement of holding a book in your hand.

Mainly, the cost is lower than its physical counterpart, the hardcover. Although they both cost money to print, paperback costs are lower. And depending on which printing option you choose, Print-on-Demand or Offset printing (more on these later in the chapter), those printing costs could get pretty high, cutting deep into your royalties. So it's important to factor in printing costs—the publishing industry's version of cost of goods sold (COGS).

Having a paperback option also opens additional possibilities in your marketing plan. Things like Goodreads giveaways and book signings aren't possible without a physical book.

At Visionary Literary, we don't publish e-books without publishing paperbacks as well. We work with thought leaders looking to enhance their credibility and authority in their field. You can't do that with an e-book alone. I would suggest the same for you: include, at the very least, a paperback format when you publish.

HARDCOVER

Choosing to publish a hardcover format is more of an individual decision than anything else. Some people like to have it as an option because it adds to the credibility of your book. Others know their target readers like to collect dust jackets. There can be a variety of reasons to choose a hardcover option.

The process is a little more costly because your hardcover binding costs more to print, but Print-on-Demand (POD) options allow authors to publish in this format.

What you should consider at this point, when determining whether to choose a hardcover option or not, is there will be additional costs incurred up front, before printing costs.

A new cover design will need to be created—one that is required for a dust jacket with flaps on the front and back cover. The trim size of the book will be different, too, so you will need a new interior file. In addition, you will need another ISBN, as a new one is needed for each format in which you publish your book.

Yes, that's a lot. However, hardcovers can be collector's items. After all, they sit much nicer on a bookshelf than a paperback. They look clean, neat, and the corners of the cover don't get frayed the way paperbacks do.

AUDIOBOOK

If you're writing a nonfiction business book, there's no doubt you've listened to an audiobook or podcast. Consuming content while multitasking is becoming a thing of importance. We're constantly crunching time yet we simultaneously want to expand our minds with valuable content.

Having an audiobook available can be a great option for your readers, but it will come at a cost. Creating an audiobook means more than just creating a new cover design. You need to decide whether you want to narrate the book yourself or hire voiceover talent.

If you choose the first, you need to ensure you have the proper equipment. Your basic, internal microphone on your laptop or computer won't suffice. You need an external microphone—a good one. You need to soundproof your room with studio foam. And proper software will be required to listen, edit, and adjust the content.

If you choose to hire talent, you need to make sure the talent's voice matches your book. How clear is the voice talent in their speaking? What do they sound like? Does their tone match the tone presented in the written version(s) of your book?

Publishing an audiobook can create a fair amount of additional work, but it can be worth it. Remember when we discussed your goal for the book back in Chapter 4? If publishing an audiobook helps you to achieve that goal, then go for it. That being said, it certainly isn't required.

OFFSET PRINTING VERSUS PRINT ON-DEMAND (POD)

These terms are important to know when it comes to paperback and hardcover versions of your book. Mostly, they have to do with whether you buy your books in bulk and resell them, or you make your book available to be printed at the time it is ordered.

First is Print-on-Demand, or POD. This option is the reason self-publishing has been attainable for anybody. With a POD option, there is little up-front cost associated. You can list your book through a distributor (more detail in the next chapter), and you don't need to pay for the printing costs until the book is ordered and printed.

Say, for example, your book is listed on Amazon. The book's price is $12.99. When someone orders your book, it is then put into a queue and printed by Amazon. Only then will you be charged for the printing costs, and they will be subtracted from the price the reader paid for your book. If the printing costs are $9.25, then the remaining royalty for the book is $3.74, which is divided between you and the publisher—Amazon, in this example.

Offset Printing is different. This is printing in bulk. Publishers do this to drive down costs, and you have the option to do so, too.

You know how this works. You've done it with your marketing materials and business merchandise. The more you order, the lower the cost per unit.

The problem with self-publishing this way is you need to warehouse the books somewhere. If you order 5,000 books to drive down the cost-per-unit, you could be stuck with 5,000 books in your garage. Or you will be stuck with a monthly warehousing bill if you store your books elsewhere (many offset printing companies offer these warehouse services).

Which one is best? That will depend on how hands-on you want to be. Do you want Amazon to do all the work and sell your books for you? Or do you want to print in bulk, sign up with a Seller account on Amazon, and package and ship the book orders yourself?

The distribution options in the next chapter should help to answer that question.

CHAPTER 16

DISTRIBUTION

"If opportunity doesn't knock, build a door."

— *Milton Berle*

YOUR BOOK IS FINALIZED, you've determined which formats you wish to publish, and the layout has been created for each. Now you're ready to set up your book for distribution to all the major retailers, so your readers can buy your book to read.

Since you have chosen to retain creative control and self-publish, you have the ability to distribute your book globally. That means a listing on websites like Amazon, Barnes & Noble, Books-A-Million, IndieBound, Audible, and almost every other book retailer on the planet. If they sell books, they can sell *your* book.

Distribution channels used to only be available to the big,

traditional publishing houses. This was, again, due to high costs that self-publishers—even smaller publishers—couldn't afford.

Technology has rapidly changed this and made it possible to publish and distribute. It's even caused traditional distributors to open their doors to the everyday individual who wants to publish a book. IngramSpark, for example, is the self-publishing arm of Ingram Books, which distributes traditionally published titles globally.

A little company called Amazon offers some amazing distribution as well.

Both distributors, Amazon and IngramSpark, allow you to get your book into every retailer's online catalog, making it possible for anyone to quickly order it online. Here's how to set up your title for distribution with each format.

E-BOOK

To get your e-book distributed on every e-reader platform, you can upload your file onto nearly every e-reader's self-service platform. If you use lots of images in your book and your file size is large, it might be best to upload to each individual e-reader. But the easiest process is to use both Amazon and IngramSpark. This will get you all the distribution you need.

Let's start with Amazon.

Amazon's KDP, or Kindle Direct Publishing, is their self-publishing platform. To create a book, you will need to sign up for their platform. From there, it's incredibly simple. The site will walk you through the entire setup process. There will be a place to upload your cover image, your interior .epub file, insert a title, subtitle, select categories, place keywords, write your description, and any other book information.

One thing you will want to be aware of is the KDP Select option. By choosing this option, you get added perks like being enrolled in some Amazon-exclusive programs. But remember that these are exclusive to Amazon, which means your e-book must be exclusive to Kindle. By enrolling in KDP Select, you must not have your e-book available anywhere else.

If you're okay with being exclusive to Amazon, this is a great program to join. If not, steer clear of the KDP Select option to avoid trouble down the road. And don't worry, you still get the same great, professional Amazon listing someone enrolled in KDP Select would get.

To publish to other e-readers, you will want to go through IngramSpark. The process here is similar: sign up for an account, upload your files, input all of your information, and submit.

IMPORTANT: When selecting e-reader platforms within the IngramSpark distribution network, make sure you **deselect Amazon**. By listing on both Amazon natively and through IngramSpark's network, you could end up with a duplicate listing.

Why is this bad? Think of how critical it could be to receive the first ten or twenty reviews on your book. If they are split up, half being submitted to one listing and the other half to another listing, you are seriously hurting your chances for higher rankings and the potential for bestseller status. Plus, it just looks unprofessional.

PAPERBACK

Amazon's KDP began as an e-book only platform, but has since added a paperback option for your book. This places your paperback book for availability on Amazon and, even better, enrolls it in Amazon Prime. Your book can now be delivered to a reader's doorstep the day after they order it online.

After submitting your Kindle version, you will be able to convert that Kindle version into a paperback format. The setup process is just as simple for the paperback as it is for the e-book.

For every other book retailer—Barnes & Noble, Books-A-Million, and thousands of other retailers—you need to go through IngramSpark. One major difference here is that there is a one-time setup fee for your book. At the time of this book's publication, that fee is $25 for the paperback version.

IMPORTANT: For every update to your files, another charge will be incurred. For example, if you decide to change your Author Bio section six months after publication to match your current social media handles or business endeavors, you will need to upload a new interior file. This action will trigger another $25 fee. More importantly, it could de-list your book (or show a status of *Out of Stock*) while the changes are reviewed and processed.

ALSO IMPORTANT: Remember, again, to **deselect Amazon** to avoid a duplicate listing.

HARDCOVER

The world of self-publishing has had some incredibly rapid advancements, but hardcover print options have yet to completely catch up. This is especially true for the POD options.

Only recently has Amazon enabled a hardcover feature, but there are limitations. Trim sizes and the option to have a dust jacket are two of Amazon's limitations for nonfiction titles. As of this writing, Amazon only offers *case laminate* covers, which are the type of hardcovers you see on textbooks or children's books.

Cloth covers with dust jackets, which is how most nonfiction hardcover titles print today, aren't an option with Amazon. Not yet, anyway. Again, these changes have become rapid and if Amazon sees the benefit in offering cloth hardcover options with dust jackets, they will certainly find a way to offer them.

Hardcover options for dust jackets with dust covers *are* available on IngramSpark, though. And they can be distributed through Amazon. The same process for setting up a paperback title applies here—interior files and cover files need to be uploaded and a fee will be applied with each new upload after initial approval.

What about Amazon Prime? That depends on whether IngramSpark chooses to be enrolled in the program. If so, your book can be available. But if not, your book—as well as every other hardcover offered through IngramSpark—will not be available for Prime.

AUDIOBOOK

The audiobook publishing process is much more in-depth than the written book process because the audio hasn't yet been created. The words have been written, but they haven't been converted to a spoken audio file.

Working with a site like Amazon Creation Exchange (ACX) offers you an all-in-one platform: voice talent, production, and publication. And they list your book on sites outside of Amazon as well. Publishing through ACX means distribution to Audible, Amazon, and iTunes.

If you want a wider range of distribution, sites like Findaway Voices or Author's Republic can get you into a larger distribution pool. Of course, ACX might also expand its distribution list after this book has been written and published, so be sure to check their website to see the current distribution list.

YOUR DISTRIBUTION OPTIONS

It has been incredible to witness how technology has sent the publishing world into overdrive. The previous chapters are proof that you hold the keys in your hand. Retaining complete creative control as a self-published author allows you to distribute to whichever channels you wish, in whichever formats you wish.

Which ones are right for you? Speak with your team, refer back to your target reader, and determine the right path for you. And remember that creative control means being able to do whatever you choose. Want to release e-book and paperback only for the time being? Go ahead. Roll out the hardcover and audiobook over time if you'd like. You have the power.

Need some assistance determining formats best aligned with the goal for your book? Head to www.visionaryliterary.com/diy-resources—or use the QR code below—to be taken to a checklist we use with our authors.

CHAPTER 17

PRICING

"Price is what you pay. Value is what you get."

— *Warren Buffett*

NOW THAT YOU have an idea of which book formats to choose and the printing costs of each, how will you price your book? Is it best to price based on what you wish to earn on each copy sold? Should you focus on what your competitor pricing structure looks like? Or should you price your book on the low end to gain more sales and, subsequently, more reviews?

The tactics vary based on the goal for your book, discussed in Chapter 4. And we'll get into some of those strategies for pricing. But first, let's clarify the traditional pricing structure for book sales, as used by traditional book publishers of all levels.

THE TRADITIONAL BUSINESS MODEL

Book sales create revenue. That's the model for publishers. Without book sales, there is no revenue. Without revenue, there is no business. Sales numbers become the primary ambition.

This is why the process of cutting costs is so important within the publishing business. Publishers use offset printing methods instead of print-on-demand because offset printing cuts costs. Royalties for each sale are then a bit higher. Each sale adds more to their bottom line if they use the offset printing model.

They also have a strategic book release model that allows them to maximize profits: they release the version with the highest profit margin first. For example, hardcover books come with a higher price tag. Consumers know this, and they are okay with it. Hardcovers are usually the first to be released, meaning supporters of the author and those truly excited about the new book will pay the higher price for the book.

Works of fiction excel in this model. Think of Stephen King or J.K. Rowling and their large fanbases. When they release a new title, those fans don't care what the price is. They will pay. Publishers know this and rather than release all book formats at once, they stick to the format that earns them the greatest return. For the first few months of a book's release, this is the only version they will make available.

Then, they slowly release other copies over time. Once the initial craze has slowed a bit, the publisher will release the second-highest profit-earner. This will depend on the title and the strategy for each book, but for this example, let's say the next format on the list is the e-book. It will be released and given time to accumulate as many sales as it can before that craze slows. Next will be the paperback, and then the audiobook.

For book publishers, everything revolves around sales. And there's nothing wrong with that. It's their business model. You are certainly familiar with business models—you have one yourself.

But when *you* publish, the traditional publishers' business model won't be the model of choice.

YOUR MONETIZATION STRATEGY

Your book doesn't need to sell a million copies to be considered a financial success. Your book only needs to act as a strategic business card. It's there to prove your credibility to potential customers and clients. Your book demonstrates your expertise in a niche market.

For you, a million-dollar return could come in the form of one new client converting to your business after reading the book. (Traditional publishers don't have that luxury.)

Don't worry about pricing the book to monetize. Worry about pricing the book to sell. It sounds simple, but there's a happy medium you must find.

Price too low and your book screams *amateur*. The anchoring effect will come into play. This is the idea that a reference point is used when a potential reader is considering buying your book. Their brain will immediately turn to a similar book they have read and the price that was paid for its purchase.

For example, if you price your e-book at $1.99 when all other competitors are between $4.99 and $9.99, cognitive bias will kick in for the potential reader, and they will have a negative assumption of your book. They don't even need to read the description. It's all in the price.

Pricing too high has the same effect. Ever come across a hardcover listed online for somewhere in the high thirty-dollar range? Your eyes lit up, didn't they? That price is way too high compared to a normal hardcover book.

Your monetization strategy is all about growing your business—this book is just a tool for doing so. You need to price your books correctly, but you don't need to worry about pinching pennies to add to your bottom line. The business you will gain from being a published author will do that.

YOUR PRICING STRUCTURE

To price your books, do a quick search on Amazon for your competitors. If you're unsure of who they are or which books are available, search by keyword and see what comes up. The beauty of the internet is research can be done in a matter of minutes. No library or bookstore visits needed.

At Visionary Literary, we help clients publish books through their own name or LLC, or we let them use our publishing imprint, Springboard Publishing, while still retaining complete control. It all depends on their future plans for the book and brand.

What we have found while working with these clients is there are certain ranges that work well.

E-BOOK

E-book prices for most nonfiction books work well at $4.99, regular price (*more on promotional techniques in Part 5*). Distributors like Amazon and IngramSpark give a 70 percent royalty rate for books between $2.99 and $9.99 and this sits right in the sweet spot.

PAPERBACK

Physical books are harder to put a solidified price range on because there are printing costs that come into play. For example, pricing a 100-page book at $10.99 will earn you a much higher royalty than pricing a 300-page book at $10.99. To be honest, the print-on-demand cost for a 300-page book might even be greater than $10.99, so you wouldn't be able to price it that low.

The price for your paperback depends on page count, weight and color of the paper being used, ink color, and the cover type (matte or glossy). These printing costs and the distributor's royalty fee will determine what you earn for each sale.

This is one reason why we aim for a 35,000-word manuscript with our clients. With our chosen typesetting and interior layout style, this brings the page count to roughly 240 pages. With a price tag of $13.99, which is right in the middle of the pack for a nonfiction paperback, a 240-page paperback can earn a royalty for the author of about $4.50.

HARDCOVER

Hardcover books are more expensive to print, but the cost can be offset by dropping the page count. Both typesetting and trim size can allow this to happen. It takes a bit of trial and error to make the combination work but if you can get to a point where your hardcover is between $18.99 and $21.99, you are in a great position.

This, of course, could depend upon your specific industry. But a hardcover at 220 pages with black and white ink on basic, white paper with a price tag of $19.99 could net you a roughly $3.75 royalty.

AUDIOBOOK

Audiobook pricing somewhat varies since monthly subscriptions are available in exchange for credits, but the prices still have some technical aspect. According to Audible, audiobooks are typically priced based on recorded length.

A book that takes less than an hour to listen to from start to finish is usually priced at under $7. That price rises to a range of $7 to $10 for a one- to three-hour book. For three to five hours, $10 to $20. Five to ten hours, $15 to $25. Ten to twenty hours, $20 to $30. And anything over twenty hours usually costs between $25 and $35.

How long will your audiobook be? The typical range for books we work on is about five hours of narrated content. This leaves your audiobook's price falling somewhere near the $17 to $22 range.

PRICING TIP TO SELL YOUR DESIRED FORMAT

It's normal to have a favorite format to sell. If you're the leader of a business with nine-figure sales numbers, you may not want your e-books being the top seller. You may prefer to have hardcovers flying off the (virtual) shelves.

If you're a course creator whose book is more of a workbook than anything else, you may desire a small, portable paperback to be your top selling format. This would allow your reader to have it with them at all times.

It doesn't matter which format you wish to sell more. Whichever your choice, you can create a pricing strategy that helps push potential readers toward the format of your choosing.

Let's say you run a successful small business you inherited from a parent. Pretend, for this example, that the transition was strenuous. There was a lot of fighting amongst your family, lawyers needed to get involved, and times were tough.

Yet now, in hindsight, you see the problems that took place, and you have been coaching other family-owned businesses on their succession plan. Your business caters to senior executives and business leaders, and you want your book to be something they can place on their bookshelf and be reminded of from time to time, so hardcover is the format of choice.

With this being the case, you want to keep your hardcover book at the low end of the mid-range price chart: $17.99, which earns you a roughly $2.50 royalty. But you aren't worried about the royalty, you're worried about the book lasting for years and years on personal bookshelves.

Using the above example, let's say you have a pricing structure like this:

E-book: $2.99
Paperback: $11.99
Hardcover: $17.99
Audiobook: $22.99

They're good prices, but you aren't enticing the potential reader to buy your hardcover. The e-book looks too cheap to pass up. They might be more tempted to read the e-book and tell themselves that they'll buy the hardcover if the book seems worth it. (But how many people actually follow through with that?) Plus, the paperback version is much cheaper and for only a few dollars more, they can have the luxury of owning the audiobook.

What you should do instead is price like this:

E-book: $8.99
Paperback: $15.99
Hardcover: $17.99
Audiobook: $25.99

Here, the potential buyer will do a bit of thinking to see which format has the best value. The e-book seems pricey compared to other formats. For an additional two dollars, they can have a hardcover instead of a paperback. And it would cost a bit too much for the audiobook. So the hardcover—your desired format to sell—is in a perfect position to sell.

There are promotional techniques to push sales, also. But for set pricing, this technique works well for selling a specific book format.

PART FIVE

MARKETING AND PROMOTION

CHAPTER 18
BOOK DESCRIPTION

"Here's the only thing you're selling, no matter what business you're in: you're selling your prospect a better version of themselves."

— Joanna Wiebe

YOU'VE DONE IT! You have written a book and published it for the world to see. It feels good, doesn't it? There's just one problem: there are roughly 750,000 books published each year *in the U.S. alone.* How are people supposed to find your book?

You can spend all the money in the world on advertising to get eyes to your book's landing page, but that doesn't guarantee sales. The material needs to convert potential readers into buyers.

If you've followed this book's guidance to this point, you've done everything you can to publish a quality book. You structured your book, wrote in an engaging fashion, created a great cover with blurbs sponsoring the content of your book. You have all the seeds planted. Now, you need to water those seeds and watch the fruits of your labor grow.

Creating a marketing plan for your book is the key to seeing that growth. We will discuss ways to promote within this section but the first and most important aspect is to have an engaging book description. It must be engaging and it must capture the attention of the reader.

But there's a catch. Your book description not only has to satisfy the human eye, it also has to satisfy computer algorithms.

THE COMPUTER ASPECT

First, the computer aspect of your book description: keywords. Everything revolves around keywords. If you're in business, you already know how important they are to your marketing efforts.

When used properly, keywords can rise you in the ranks of search engines, all the way up to the top of the first page. Used incorrectly, however—or not at all—and you could find yourself pushed down to page ten, twenty, fifty, or several hundred pages down.

Know anyone who has spent the time to go through more than two or three pages of search engine results? Me neither.

There are two ways to get onto the first page of search engine results—paid ad placement or organic search. The first you will pay for, sometimes handsomely. The second is free, but you need to use keywords tactically.

There are two things you will need to know. The first is where to find keywords. We discussed this in Chapter 11 when talking about your title, and those same websites—SEMrush, Google Keyword Planner, and Ahrefs—can be used here.

Which keywords in your industry get the most traction? How high are they on the search charts? Include some of these important, common keywords, but also remember there's a ton of competition at the top. Use some niche keywords, too. Search for the ones that only have a few hundred searches. These can give you a much better chance of getting a potential reader to your page because it brings them to something they were specifically looking for.

THE HUMAN COMPONENT

In Chapter 7, we talked about how attention spans are becoming increasingly shorter. We have so many options, and our minds are aware of this. If something doesn't seem worthwhile, we'll move along.

Certainly, you have done this on the Amazon page of some product. Maybe it was a book, maybe it wasn't. Whatever the case, something about the product's listing threw you off, and the description wasn't written well enough to compel you to buy.

If you want your book to stand out from the millions of others available to your potential reader, you need to make it stand out. An appealing cover design is a great start, but the book's description needs to seal the deal. Here's how it can do so.

- **Target your reader's pain points**. Open with this. Make the first few sentences relatable. Tell the reader that he or she is not alone in their feelings of pain, doubt, etc.

- **Explain the transformation this book will provide**. Don't provide the method, your book will do that. Simply tell the reader what their life will be like once they have read the book and implemented the strategies within.

- **Use italic and bold fonts to distinguish important text.** Most people will only skim through your text. Time is the most valuable asset for all of us, so we try to savor it. If your description is written in long, daunting paragraphs, you will almost certainly lose your potential reader.

- **Add compelling reviews at the top of your product page.** Did you receive some great reviews for your book? Or blurbs from important people or companies? Highlight those at the top of your book's description on the product

page. Excite your potential buyer from the very
first sentence.

WRITING A GREAT DESCRIPTION

Now it's time to combine the two. Start with the human
component in mind and write a description of about 200
words that sounds appealing. Then, run through the
description and look for places where keywords can be used
in place of the natural text.

Be careful here not to "keyword stuff" your description.
Once again, Chapter 11 touched on this and how Amazon
could penalize your title for doing so, and it can begin to
sound ridiculous. Avoid keyword stuffing at all costs.

Plus, will someone really be enticed to buy a book with a
spammy description? Sure, keyword stuffing might get your
book to the top of a search engine result, but that doesn't
matter if nobody is buying. Actually, according to Amazon's
search engine algorithm, a book page with many clicks and
few purchases will be pushed lower in the rankings. To
Amazon, that combination is a red flag.

Want some inspiration? Search for bestselling books and
read through their descriptions. Then, go deep into the
rankings and look at descriptions of books that aren't selling.
That should give you a good idea of where to begin.

OUTSOURCING YOUR DESCRIPTION

Description writing versus book writing—there's a definite difference. In marketing, it's called copywriting versus content writing. They are two completely different methods of writing. Don't get discouraged if it takes you days or weeks to finally settle on a 200-word book description.

But I could write 200 words in my manuscript in less than an hour!

I know. Believe me, I know. Creative writing and copywriting are two different things. Copywriting, as you know from your business's marketing efforts, is all about selling. And selling just comes naturally to some while others struggle with it.

If you know the content inside your book is helpful but you're struggling with the sales aspect, one option you have is to hire. Luckily, the process to hire a writer today is quick and simple. **Reedsy**, **Upwork**, or even **Fiverr** can provide you with wide pools of talent from which to select.

I know Upwork and Fiverr have been mentioned as having lower-tier writers, but they do have some good writers as well. And since you're only paying someone to write about 200 words, the trial and error window doesn't seem so narrow.

The most important thing to know about your book's description is you can change it at any time. There are no fees associated with it. You won't be penalized by search engines. You can change your book's description at your leisure to match trending keywords or topics. So don't stress over this part too much. (At the same time, don't simply throw something together.)

With your book description written, you are now in a much better position to move forward. What you need next is a marketing plan. Yes, an entire marketing plan, just like you created for your business.

CHAPTER 19

CREATING YOUR PLAN

"If you don't know where you are going, you'll end up someplace else."

— *Yogi Berra*

DO you remember the early days of your business? Back when everything was up in the air, exciting, and you often wondered what the hell you were doing—*is this really going to work?*

But you followed your dream anyway. You created some sort of plan, whether it was a business plan, marketing plan, or both. And that plan gave you, at the very least, a flashlight to have along your dark and unknown path.

You are about to travel a similar, unknown path again. And you'll definitely need a flashlight, especially if you are a first-time author.

WHEN TO BEGIN

You need a marketing plan for your book, but when should you start initiating this plan? When do the wheels start turning?

That will vary by project. What I can tell you now is this:

It's never too early, but it *can* be too late. Here's what I mean...

IT'S NEVER TOO EARLY

Every author stumbles through the process of writing. At some point or another, a roadblock is hit. Something stops you and that transforms the process from a fun project to a daunting task. It's inevitable. This is too long of a project to operate smoothly for its duration.

You begin with the planning, then you outline, next comes the first draft, then the edits, the reviews—it's a lot of work. (The eighteen chapters before this are proof.)

If you give yourself a reason to walk away, it becomes much easier to do so. This is especially true if you're a solopreneur working alone on your book. Without a team around you to keep you on track and to help keep the process moving forward, any small hiccup could turn into something much greater.

You can still have a support system around you without having a team. This support system comes in the form of what people in the publishing industry call your *street team*. Who are the people that know you're writing a book and are truly excited about it? Who are your—or your company's— superfans? Is it family and friends? Clients? Colleagues? Any of these are good candidates.

Bring this street team into the process early. Announce to them you're writing a book and continue to build excitement. As the book progresses, you can build from their excitement. You will then gain the confidence to start sharing announcements with larger groups: on social media, within the company, to extended family and friends.

Bringing people into the process with you relieves you of that loneliness most self-published authors feel. If you're a solopreneur, you know this feeling all too well. It can be a drain on your motivation.

BUT IT CAN BE TOO LATE

The earlier, the better is a simple solution for some people. But it's not ideal for everyone. Maybe you have multiple projects in the works, or you want this book to be a side project. Maybe you don't want deadlines and you simply want to get started and get a feel for the process before diving in head first.

I get that. I don't think I've ever had an initial call with a client who *didn't* have some sort of hesitation about the process. That's normal. So it's okay to take your time, especially in the beginning stages.

But remember this: going at it alone makes it too easy to

walk away. There's no accountability. No support. No team around you. How many successful companies do you know that operate with a one-person team?

When the bad days come—and, again, they will—going at it alone without anyone knowing what you're working on makes it too easy to call it quits. If there is no street team to promote what you're doing, no family or friends to encourage you, and no moral support from an advisory board or group of colleagues, your bad days will make you feel like you're attempting to write this book for nothing.

Don't allow this to happen. Think of all the people who need your book. Think about *you*—about the you from ten or twenty years ago whose life and career could have taken off if given this information.

If there's ever a doubt in your mind as you go through this journey, remember your past self and others like you. If you write for no one else, write for them.

AN ADDITIONAL NOTE ON TIMING AND 'WHEN TO BEGIN'

You have to walk a line between announcing your book idea and sharing too much information. On one hand, subtle announcements that come only every few weeks and with no supporting information to drive excitement won't get you anywhere. You need to give people a glimpse into what you're working on.

On the other hand, sharing too much too early could prove to backfire. You don't want to open the doors and make this project a public forum. Think of this process as sneak peeks, not open collaboration.

One example of what not to do is to share first draft material. For example, if you've just written a great chapter and you want to share that as a "sneak peek" blog post, have someone tie you to a chair and don't let them untie you for several hours—not until the excitement subsides.

Why? Because it isn't ready for the world yet. Don't share any content until it's finalized. I'm talking editorial review, subsequent drafts complete—heck, even waiting until the typesetting process has been done so you *know* nothing will change.

Because that's the worrisome part: *change*. What if you share that "great chapter" and there are spelling errors you didn't notice. Or the context is fuzzy. The structure is out of whack. The voice adjusts back and forth from past tense to present (because, after all, it's just a draft).

If you're excited about a brilliant writing session, that's fantastic. Share *that* news—*Hey, everyone! Just had a great writing session. Cannot wait to share this book with you!*

Excite people while keeping secrecy intact. It will prove to be far more valuable in the long run.

WHERE TO BEGIN

Alright, enough about a timeline, what to share, when to say it, and so forth. Let's talk about actionable tasks. How can you get started with creating a professional marketing plan for your book?

You've done this before. As a business owner or industry leader, you have dealt with marketing plans in the past. If you have a marketing expert on your team or have used templates in the past, you can probably skip right over this section.

If you don't have that sort of team around you, there are still plenty of options. There's technology all around us and a marketing plan can be created in just a few short hours using some of the templates available.

Where to find marketing plan templates:

- **Canva.** This is a free online tool that has thousands of templates to choose from. And they aren't bare, old formats. They are created using sleek graphic design and are intended for professionals looking to display a high level of professionalism.

- **Microsoft Word.** Word also has marketing plan templates from which to choose. While the design might not be Canva-esque, it still looks professional and has the appropriate formatting to get the job done.

- **Visionary Literary Resources.** We have put together a list of important documents you will need for do-it-yourself book writing, publishing, and promoting at www.visionaryliterary.com/diy-resources. At the conclusion of the next chapter, you will find a specific link that brings you to our marketing plan template—the one we use with our clients. This can be a great starting point for your own promotional plan.

CHAPTER 20

THE COMPONENTS OF YOUR PLAN

"By failing to prepare, you are preparing to fail."

— *Benjamin Franklin*

THERE'S a lot that can go into your plan. A *lot*. And the ingredients of your plan will vary based on your industry, the goal for your book, and your advertising budget.

For instance, a Goodreads book giveaway might be a great idea for an entrepreneur who has created a consumer product because it gets their book (and product) in front of consumers. (More on this in a bit.)

An industry leader or course creator looking to book public speaking gigs at national conferences, however, wouldn't benefit from this. Their target reader is a busy organizer who receives hundreds if not thousands of unsolicited queries for speaking engagements. They're not browsing Goodreads for the next book giveaway.

Everything with your marketing plan begins back in Part 1 of this book. *What is your 'why'? What is the goal? Who is your target audience?* These will also define which pieces you use to construct your plan.

What's provided below is meant to be the ground floor of your marketing plan. It includes the most general—but *essential*—components of a nonfiction book's marketing plan. I will lay it out here in timeline fashion.

SIX-PLUS WEEKS TO BOOK LAUNCH

CREATE YOUR PLAN

First thing's first: **create your plan**. Use the template I'll provide at the end of this chapter—or use one of the many templates available on Canva or Microsoft Word. As Mark Twain said, "The secret of getting ahead is getting started."

Your business didn't start to grow until you put something into action, right? Your business plan, advertising, funding—something had to happen to get the ball rolling. Creating your plan is your first move.

ANNOUNCE YOUR PROJECT

Grab your megaphone—or, in the 21st century, your cell phone—and shout to the world. Announce your project.

Tell family, friends, business associates, and clients about your new endeavor.

In a short, sweet message to your social media networks and/or email list, announce your book. More importantly, tell your following how the book will benefit them. Get them excited for its potential to impact their lives.

PODCAST OUTREACH

Which podcasts do your target audience members listen to? Where do your potential clients get their information? Begin doing some research into which places you can make a name for yourself, either as an advertiser on the podcast or as a guest. (Or both. Some podcasts offer discounted deals for advertisers after you have been a guest.)

Start contacting these shows. In a short message, tell them who you are, inform them of your book's upcoming release, and give two or three bulleted ideas of what can be discussed on the show, if you are to be a guest.

Ideally, you will want to have these appearances booked for the week of the book's release, but any time after is fine. Not before, though. You don't want to waste your time on a podcast telling listeners to "keep an eye out for the book!" That won't bode well for you. (Unless you have an active pre-order.)

FOUR WEEKS TO LAUNCH

CREATE A LANDING PAGE

Have you purchased the domain name for your book yet? If not, **Bluehost** or **GoDaddy** are two places to check availability.

If the domain name is available for your book, purchase it. For example, if your book is titled *XYZ for Beginners*, purchase the domain *XYZforBeginners.com*. This will be the link you can use when promoting your book at any stage of its life—pre-publication, launch, and post-launch.

Search engines will be happier if you do the above process of purchasing the domain that matches your book title, but you can also create a page on your current website. Say your book title, *XYZ for Beginners*, is the same title as your business and you already have a website set up using *XYZforBeginners.com*. You can create a page —*XYZforBeginners.com/book*, for example—within your domain.

If your book name doesn't match your business name, you can still use the subpage method. But be sure to include the title of the book in that page's URL to help with search engine optimization (SEO).

Search engines give higher value to keywords that are farther left in the URL, though, meaning a site like XYZforBeginners.com will rank higher than yourbusinessdomain.com/XYZforBeginners. If possible, buying the domain name is the preferred method.

On the landing page, have an image of your book with an email opt-in form and, when the book is available, links to sites where the book is being sold.

BEGIN TO TEASE THE BOOK

Once your manuscript has been finalized—edited, proofread, locked, and ready for the world to see—start sharing small pieces on your social media channels and to your email list. You will get a chance to share an entire chapter in the future, but for now, it's all about small things —a powerful few sentences, a quote, or an image.

Do you know what's even better than simply sharing a sentence or two? Share the story behind those meaningful sentences. Create a short video and discuss the meaning behind them. Show the potential readers who you are as a person. Be humble.

If you have your book cover design completed by this point, share that, too. When you introduce your book, having a cover image helps to make it tangible. Don't just post the rectangular cover image, though. Use a mockup image site like **DIYBookCovers** or **SmartMockups** to create professional images.

SEND OUT ARCS

ARCs, or Advanced Reader Copies of your book, are early copies of the book sent out to influencers who can provide valuable feedback or write up an article before the book's release. They can leave reviews, blurbs, and give public forms of feedback. Their credibility, and audience, can help to sell your book.

Who receives ARCs? Start with those podcasters you're reaching out to for booking. Send a copy to the host (and an additional copy or two for the production team). This is highly recommended if you're going to be a guest on the show. Granted, you'll be promoting your business, but sending a copy of your book helps to add credibility before the interview.

ARCs can also be sent to influencers. Who are the leading voices in your industry? Who is on Linkedin making the most noise and capturing the most attention in your space? Will their admiration for your work help expose your book to more potential readers? Reach out to them and ask to send an ARC copy in exchange for a review—an *honest* review.

What about media companies? ABC, FOX, and CNN might have rules against unsolicited mail and email so sending to these channels might lead to disappointment. If you have a connection within a media network, try to use that connection. Otherwise, it might not be the greatest use of your team's time.

The best part about ARC copies in the 21st century?

They're digital, meaning they're free. No printing costs and no shipping costs. Only a decade or so ago, before sending digital ARCs was acceptable, this was a costly process. You would need to pay for printing and shipping costs for every ARC sent out. It would be disheartening when people wouldn't respond.

That's no longer the case. Everything is digital (unless, of course, someone requests a physical copy).

IMPORTANT: When you create an ARC to send, make sure it has "this is an Advanced Reader Copy" somewhere in the front matter of the book. For digital files, you can even place it in the header of every page. In the event something inside the book changes between the time the reader consumes the content and the public version is published, this gives an explanation as to why.

TWO WEEKS TO LAUNCH

KEYWORDS AND CATEGORIES

How will you be found and how will you be ranked? Keywords and categories will determine each. That means going through this step isn't about guesswork. It's about research, planning, and the same A/B testing you have been using to market your business or product line.

With two weeks to go, make sure your book is categorized in the correct places, and you want to give sites time to update this. With Amazon, any changes to description, categories, or keywords can be seen almost instantaneously. But with

IngramSpark, time may vary for this information to get to each of their channels.

Keywords and categories are input at the time you set up your title—this is true on both IngramSpark and Amazon—but can be changed at any time (no costs included).

The difference between categories and keywords is this:

Categories are the topics under which your book can be placed. *Marketing and Advertising* could be a category. *Self-Help. Autobiographies and Memoirs.* They are broad but they explain where your book would be placed inside of a bookstore.

Keywords are the phrases people will use to search for your book. These are descriptions of your book. *Self-help book for recent college graduates* could be a keyword. *How to sell a business* could be another. These aren't sections you would see in any bookstore, but they are phrases people would type into a search bar to look for their next read.

Having your book placed in the wrong category could hurt your book's ranking, so make sure you properly categorize your title.

Incorrect keywords can do the same. If your book about marketing to millennials has the keyword *a detailed history of nonfiction books*, people who type *a detailed history of nonfiction books* might come across your title in the search results, but it won't be what they're looking to read. That will lower your title's conversion rate, ultimately pushing it down farther in rankings and making it more difficult to find for those who *do* want to read it.

CREATE YOUR 'AMAZON AUTHOR' PAGE

There's always talk around promoting your books on social media—I've done it here, too. The important thing about social media is it allows others to connect with you on a personal level. People can skim through your profile and know more about you without ever even meeting you. It's an important tool to use when promoting yourself, your business, or your book.

The same can be said about an Amazon Author page. Amazon's **Author Central** allows any author to set up a page on their site. Doing so allows potential readers to know a little more about you and to follow you, getting alerts when you upload a new piece of work.

For you, the author, Author Central allows you to list all your titles on one page, but it also lets you build an email list specifically for those who want to read your books. And when you release a new piece of work onto Amazon's site, they will automatically push out a notification to anyone who follows your Author Central page—no additional work required.

ONE WEEK TO LAUNCH

CONTINUED SOCIAL MEDIA POSTS

In the beginning, your social media plan consisted of sharing excerpts of your book on your channels. You gave potential readers insight into the process, giving them the *backstage pass* feeling. That helped to keep people continuously engaged.

Now, with only one week to go before launch, it's time to move to the social proof concept. That is, get people excited about your book by showing how excited *other* people were about reading your book.

Remember those blurbs on your book cover or on the first few pages of your book? Use those as social media posts. A simple method can be one blurb per day. And if you don't have blurbs, you can use early reviews from those that have responded positively to the ARC you sent them.

SCHEDULE A GOODREADS GIVEAWAY

Goodreads is a social media website that allows readers to share their reading history, review books, and find new authors. You, as the author, can take advantage of this site by setting up a page with Goodreads and setting up a book giveaway. You can do so with digital copies or with print copies.

Goodreads giveaways work by offering a free giveaway of a specific number of books to anyone who participates in the contest. Say, for example, you are giving away five free books and the giveaway ends in 72 hours. Within those 72 hours, anybody who adds your book as "To Read" on their digital bookshelf will be included in the raffle that takes place at the end.

When the 72 hours ends, Goodreads automatically chooses the winner(s) and sends you a message. If the giveaway is for print copies, you (or your team) will be responsible for shipping those books by a specified date.

The benefit of this giveaway is that you will typically get hundreds of people marking your book as "To Read," meaning your book is on their reading list. And since Goodreads works like a social media network, others can see that those people have marked your book as "To Read" and may be intrigued to check out the book themselves.

LAUNCH WEEK

SOCIAL MEDIA

There it is again: social media. But there's a reason I keep going back to this—and why every business and brand turns to it: It's free. On top of that, everybody is on it. So it's important to utilize it.

The strategy now, during the book's release week, is to include links in each of your posts. The idea behind this is to make it easy for a potential reader to buy your book. The less work they need to do, the better chance they will get to your book's page.

Don't post online, "My book is available now! Go to Amazon, Barnes and Noble, or wherever books are sold to get it!"

That won't convert. Again, make it easy: "My book is available now!" Then insert the desired link where they can buy with one click. Don't take them down a rabbit hole. Try to abide by the *three-click rule*—that the chances of a shopper converting to a sale decrease with each additional click after three.

EMAIL NEWSLETTER

This is the fun part. You have been building up your business's email lists for weeks, months, or even years. The subscribers know a book is coming, and they're excited to read it and to learn from its contents.

Now you're able to offer them a sneak peek. Write an opening piece to the subscriber, as you would any other newsletter. Then, include the opening piece of your introduction or another powerful piece from your book. It only needs to be a few paragraphs, but it should be engaging and should leave the subscriber wanting more.

What should you include at the end of the sample piece? You guessed it: a link to where they can buy.

ASK FOR REVIEWS

In the days following the launch, follow up with your email list, social networks, and others who have read the book and ask for reviews. This is important because there are certain advertising paths you can tap into—BookBub, BuckBooks, BooksButterfly being some good ones—that won't allow you to promote your book if you have fewer than ten reviews.

If you want to continually promote your book, reviews will be important. Plus, a study by the data collection company *Nielsen* found that 92 percent of consumers trust word of mouth marketing over ads.

When it comes to Amazon, reviews also help push you up the rankings. But what you really want to strive for are *verified reviews*, which are reviews from people who Amazon can verify have purchased your book through their site. If a regular review counts as an A toward your rankings grade on Amazon, a verified review is an A+.

VARIATIONS IN YOUR PLAN

There is so much that can go into your book's marketing plan. Working on your business's marketing plan has certainly given you exposure to the constant variations that will take place. Technology will continue to evolve and trends will always come and go. These are things to keep an eye on as you continue to promote your book. Don't be afraid to go outside the box and try new things.

The information included in this chapter is a good starting point to get your plan into motion. You can take this information and adjust it according to your marketing budget, your target audience, and your overall goal for your book.

The link below will take you to the template we use for each of our clients. Feel free to use this and work with your marketing team to expand upon the ideas based on your book's goals.

This document can also be found at www.visionaryliterary.com/diy-resources.

CHAPTER 21

KEEPING THE DREAM ALIVE

"The only thing that will stop you from fulfilling your dreams is you."

— *Tom Bradley*

BY THIS POINT, you've probably forgotten that you've written a book, haven't you? All this marketing talk has pushed its way to the front of the line, and the book and its contents have slowly faded into the crowd.

So let's go back to the book for a minute. Back to what made you want to write it in the first place. Your *why*.

This idea came about for a reason. You want your business to grow. You want to share insight that can help others, or boost morale through a memoir sharing your journey from the bottom to the top. You want to break into the keynote speaking world or gain enough authority to start being offered board seats.

Think of all the people you can help with your book. Picture yourself and what your path to success could have looked like if you had this information a decade or two ago. Think of the years of struggles, of testing and failing and iterating, that could have been spared.

Your book can, and will, help people. So when the initial marketing push is over and the book's rankings begin to dip, which is inevitable, don't fall into the trap of feeling as though your book has run its course. It hasn't.

Every New York Times bestseller drops from the list at some point. Every Billboard Top 100 song falls out of the rankings eventually. It isn't possible to stay at the top forever.

But your book doesn't need to sit at number one on a bestseller list to make an impact. Think of all the books you have read. Were they all new releases, or did you hear about them from a colleague or by listening to a podcast?

Your book will continue to help others, but you need to still believe in it. You don't need to keep pumping money into paid advertising campaigns, but you can continue to spread the news of your book. Here are some simple methods for keeping the dream alive and ensuring your book gets into the hands of the people you've written it for.

FREE COPIES

Do you attend conferences and trade shows often? Are you a member of your local Chamber of Commerce, a meetup group, business network, or any other event with like-minded people who could benefit from your book?

Keep a few copies of the book with you wherever you go. Whether you carry a briefcase, purse, rolling luggage or anything else, keep a few books inside. If you strike up a conversation with someone and your book, or its contents, become a focal point in the conversation, talk about your book. Pull it out of your bag and hand it to the other person.

Doing this won't seem like you're pushing it on them because you were already discussing the material. It's not like you're walking up to a stranger and handing them your book. That would be unwise, from a financial standpoint especially.

But handing over a book to someone interested in the material? *That* has benefits. One, it's a free book for that person—and who doesn't love a free book? Plus, you already know the person is interested in the contents of the book. So when they read it and find it helpful, they will be more than happy to share their positive thoughts with others who would find value in the book. Or—hopefully *and*—they will leave a glowing review online.

QR CODES AND TAPPIE

The ABCs of sales: *Always Be Closing*. You know this term from your business, sitting in meetings with your sales team. (Or maybe you *are* that sales team.)

Well here, with the book, you're not trying to sell. Because, remember, book sales aren't the ROI generator—the opportunities that arise from having a published book are. New clients, booked speaking engagements, consulting, coaching—these are the things you want to promote.

But it gets a little repetitive telling people your entire business story, doesn't it? It's why we have limited things down to the *elevator pitch*. When that elevator pitch captures someone's attention, you can direct them to your book. It's important to make this simple, though. Luckily, technology makes this doable.

The QR codes that you have seen throughout this book? Those can be generated quickly and with ease. If you use Google Chrome, all you need to do is highlight the web address in the address bar. On the right side of the bar, a QR code icon will appear. Click it, and a code will be generated.

What can you do with a QR code? How about ordering a cell phone case that has that QR code on it? When you speak with someone who is interested in your book, they can simply scan the QR code on your phone case, and they will be taken right to your website.

Don't want a phone case with a QR code on it? That's okay, there are other options. One is called **Tappie**. It's a button that sticks to the back of your phone, phone case, wallet, purse, or wherever you want it placed. When someone holds their phone up against the Tappie button, their phone will take them right to your book's page.

Remember, simplicity is key when it comes to capturing the attention of a potential reader. There are so many books, podcasts, seminars, and conferences looking to capture the attention of your target reader. Their time is limited and, unfortunately, "It's available on Amazon, go check it out," won't get them there.

USE LINKS EVERYWHERE

Include a link to your book in your bio, your email signature, on your company web page—anywhere your name lives online. This is difficult for many people because it feels too pushy, but how will people know you've written a book if you aren't telling them about it?

Think of your email signature, for instance. How many emails are sent out each day? And how many recipients are aware you have written a book?

Having visible links allows people to get to your book in a single click. If the anchor text—the blue, underlined text written in the hyperlink—is appealing, you have a much better chance of getting someone to your site than saying in plain, unlinked text, "Go to Amazon to buy my book!"

MESS WITH PRICING AND PROMOTIONS

The best part about self-publishing is you have complete control over your pricing and promotions. Do you have an event coming up and want to run a promotion for attendees? You can do that. Want to increase the hardcover price to $50 because you feel it's worth it? I'd advise against it, but you have the power to do so.

Authors who publish through traditional publishers don't have that option. They don't own the ability to price how they wish, to give away books when they desire, or to run promotions on a whim. Everything must be approved, and conducted, by the publisher.

For you, a self-published author, you can adjust prices whenever you wish. If you're looking to fill your speaking calendar for the next twelve months and need a boost, why not have a sale on paperback books and run a corresponding ad targeted toward event planners?

The options here are vast, and they are only this way because you have retained complete control over your book. Think of it as an extension of your marketing plan. It's a part of your business. You and your fellow shareholders get to determine how best to utilize it, not an outside publisher.

SCHEDULE BOOK SIGNINGS

No, you do not need to be traditionally published to have book signings. Nor do you need a Public Relations manager —although they could certainly help. As an author, you can walk into a local bookstore and ask to speak with a manager about holding a book signing.

This isn't limited to the neighborhood bookstore. You can walk into a Barnes & Noble or Books-A-Million and ask for a book signing. Depending on the manager, you may or may not be granted the ability to hold one.

There are two things a bookstore manager is looking for in an author who wishes to have a book signing at their store.

The first is how their books are published. Distributing through a major company like Ingram—which you have if you've gone through IngramSpark—is important to them because they want to know that if they order books for the event, they can return any that don't sell. Some distributors won't offer returns. (Within IngramSpark, you can choose to deny returns, too. But don't do this if you ever want bookstores to buy your books.)

For example, as you schedule your event, the manager may ask you how many books you think you can sell. If you say fifty and you only sell twenty, the bookstore is then stuck with the remaining thirty books. And they won't keep them, nor place them (not all of them, at least) on their shelves.

They want to know they can return unsold books. And when they order through IngramSpark, they can. But be careful, because returned books end up costing you money. It might only be a few dollars per copy, but those costs can add up and be counterintuitive to your book signing goals.

The second thing they want to know is how many people you can bring into their store. After all, it's a bit of work and planning to set up your free book signing.

How will the bookstore benefit from the deal? If you have a large, local social media presence and can potentially bring in an extra fifty or seventy-five people during your two-hour signing, they can see the value because those fifty or seventy-five people have the potential to make other purchases throughout the store.

KEEP DREAMING

You're an expert. A visionary. You have built something from the ground up. Ideas and motivation combined to make you the perfect person to write and share your story.

That innovative mindset is what will allow you to continually promote your book. Whether it's through writing additional books, continually improving upon ways to promote your current book, or any other form of continued marketing, you have the ability to turn this book into something incredible.

There are nearly eight billion people on this planet. Think of how many lives you can touch with your words, your wisdom, and your openness. Continue to push the envelope. Create new things. Build upon what you have.

Share your stories. Help the world. There is no better time than right now, at this very moment. At Visionary Literary, our tagline is this: *We turn experts into authors.* And through this book, I hope we have turned you, an expert in your field, into an author.

As an avid reader, I can genuinely say that I cannot wait to read your book. So please—and I truly mean this—reach out to me and let me know when you have published a book using our method. Email me directly at johnfeldman@visionaryliterary.com. Take a picture as you unbox your book and tag us on Instagram (@visionaryliterary) and let us see that new author smile.

And with that, I leave you to get started. Happy writing!

CONCLUSION

"The journey of a thousand miles begins with a single step."

— *Lao Tzu*

There's a shift in the way people are learning. College application rates have been dropping because young people everywhere are becoming aware of the benefit of self-education. Online courses, virtual learning platforms, and books have been leading the way in this shift. This trend will only continue to move toward the self-education revolution over the next decade and beyond.

By authoring a book, you not only have the ability to build your authority, but you have the ability to open the minds of young people who are about to embark on a new journey. You can open their mind to new ideas that could save them tens (or hundreds) of thousands of dollars in student loans.

It could also help them to clarify what they want out of life. And if that involves them going to college and learning more, that's great—I'm not opposed to further education.

What I *am* opposed to is the idea that everyone needs to follow a specific path: high school, college, internship, work your way up the corporate ladder. Humans don't belong in an assembly line. We all have hopes and dreams and with the tools that have become available today, we all have the capability to capture those dreams—to make a difference in the world.

By authoring a book and sharing your insight, you can positively impact people in ways you couldn't do without it. You cannot be in two places at once. You cannot operate a business and mentor hundreds, thousands, or tens of thousands of people on your own. You need help.

A book is that help. It allows you to be in multiple places at one time. You can help others while you sleep. While you work. While you spend time with your family.

TIME IS THE ONE COMMODITY WE CAN NEVER GET BACK

I've mentioned this idea of time being a scarcity quite often in this book. Clearly, it's something I feel strongly about. And what I have found in working with successful clients is that this is a shared feeling.

This book has included everything I have learned in my time rising the ranks from amateur novelist to bestselling ghostwriter. It includes the best concepts, eliminates the mistakes, and gives you the single most efficient path toward successful publication. Because, after all, when it comes to utilizing time, efficiency is key.

But there's a lot that goes into it. Clearly, as you have learned within the pages of this book, this process isn't as simple as some would make it seem. It is a long road. And you may not have the time to allocate to a project of this magnitude.

If your time is precious but you still aspire to have a book professionally written, published, and promoted, our team of writers, editors, marketers, and publishing professionals are here to help.

We have packages starting as low as $14,000 for a Publishing Only package and go higher with the more options you wish to add (a ghostwriter on your team, hardcover and audiobooks options, etc.). But every one of our packages includes professional publishing and promotion, because we want to give every author the best chance to make a difference in the world.

If your marketing budget allows for it and you don't have time to go through the steps in this book all alone, we're here to help. Use the QR code below or visit www.visionaryliterary.com/services to review our service list and see which option is best for you. Once decided, use the **Contact Us** button at the bottom of the page to get in touch with someone on our team for a free consultation to discuss best options for your project.

WRITE YOUR MASTERPIECE

I truly feel so fortunate that I was able to enter this field of writing and publishing. As a wannabe screenwriter in college, my dream was always to put on a show for the purpose of entertainment. But deep down, I always wanted to pull at peoples' emotions. I wanted to make them feel something. *Anything*.

Constant pivots in my career led me to the path of nonfiction ghostwriting, and I haven't looked back since. The book you are about to write is one that will live on forever. Long after I'm gone and you're gone, your book will be there. Although the information might not be completely relevant in fifty years—made antiquated by rapid technological enhancements—it can be a gem for your children to have. Or your grandchildren. Maybe they can take the basis of your ideas and spin them into a more modern version of truth.

My passion for this line of work and for self-education through reading is real. It shines bright. With every new book that I pick up off a shelf, or that gets delivered to my doorstep, I become a child on Christmas morning. It's why I asked you to email me and tag our company once you've published a book—because I truly, honestly want to read it and to learn from it.

As you move forward on this path to publication, I hope you become vulnerable. I hope you allow yourself to pour your heart into the pages and *feel* the value you will provide others. I hope you know just how amazing it is that you are trying to help the world and your target audience.

And I hope your business and your career thrive as a result. Because you deserve for that to happen. It isn't easy writing a book. It isn't easy opening up about failures from the past and doing something that makes you feel vulnerable.

But guess what: that vulnerability is what makes a great book. So go on and be vulnerable. Tell us everything you have to share. And I promise, we, your target reader, will be forever grateful.

John Feldman is the founder and CEO of Visionary Literary, a full-service ghostwriting, publishing, and marketing company for nonfiction authors. He started the company after a decade and a half writing, penning books for business founders, professional athletes, and industry experts.

His writing journey began as an undergraduate in college, when his late and great friend, Greg Menefee, put the idea in his head: "We should write a story about our lives."

From that project came his aha moment: *I want to be a*

writer. The journey began as an aspiring fiction author and then gained traction when he discovered his love for nonfiction books and, more importantly, the author whose names would sit in the covers of those books.

In 2021, he took his years of knowledge in the nonfiction ghostwriting, publishing, and marketing industries and put them to use.

Visionary Literary now helps authors by introducing them to 21st Century tools, simplifying the process and saving aspiring nonfiction authors the one thing they fear wasting most:

Time.